The Fundamentals of Graphic Design
Gavin Ambrose + Paul Harris

An AVA Book
Published by AVA Publishing SA
Rue des Fontenailles 16
Case Postale
1000 Lausanne 6
Switzerland
Tel: +41 786 005 109
Email: enquiries@avabooks.ch

Distributed by Thames & Hudson (ex-North America)
181a High Holborn
London WC1V 7QX
United Kingdom
Tel: +44 20 7845 5000
Fax: +44 20 7845 5055
Email: sales@thameshudson.co.uk
www.thamesandhudson.com

North American Support Office
AVA Publishing
Tel: +1 908 754 6196
Fax: +1 908 668 1172
Email: enquiries@avabooks.ch

English Language Support Office
AVA Publishing (UK) Ltd.
Tel: +44 1903 204 455
Email: enquiries@avabooks.ch

ISBN 2-940373-82-5 and 978-2-940373-82-6

10 9 8 7 6 5 4 3 2 1

Design by Gavin Ambrose

Production by AVA Book Production Pte Ltd, Singapore
Tel: +65 6334 8173
Fax: +65 6259 9830
Email: production@avabooks.com.sg

All reasonable attempts have been made to trace, clear and
credit the copyright holders of the images reproduced in this
book. However, if any credits have been inadvertently
omitted, the publisher will endeavour to incorporate
amendments in future editions.

Gavin Ambrose + Paul Harris

The Fundamentals
of Graphic Design

ava | Academia
the environment of learning

The Fundamentals of Graphic Design
———— Contents

Chloé

This space was created by Research Studios for the launch of the fragrance Chloé in Paris in 2007 and is an example of how graphic design continues to change – here, the result is the creation of a space rather than a print piece or website. It acts as a piece of environmental design and translates the values of a product into a piece that is engaging for the audience.

Contents

How to get the most out of this book

——— This book introduces various themes related to the practice of graphic design. Each chapter is illustrated with numerous examples from leading contemporary design studios, all annotated to explain how they relate to the design process.

Chapter openers
Each chapter opens with an introduction that provides a clear guide to the topic being discussed.

Chapter 6
The production process
——— This final chapter looks at the basic tool kit a graphic designer uses to create and produce effective designs. The tools unleash and channel creative ideas from the design process into workable and physical products – through the printing process or for electronic applications such as web pages. This section also includes basic information on how to ensure that control is maintained over the use of images and colour.

In-Cosmetics (opposite)
This brochure created by Research Studios helps to establish a visual identity and platform for cosmetics innovation. The use of a colourful, dreamy image alludes to how cosmetics provide a wealth of possibilities, which interact to improve the appearance of the people using them. The fine detail and the importance of image quality to the business of the client meant that high-end filled paper stock with excellent printability and colour-reception characteristics had to be used. In this example, minimal dot gain is vital to avoid registration problems. High opacity and whiteness are necessary to provide a crisp, clean background that allow the colours to reproduce as intended.

Areas looked at in this chapter
Basic tools p.150 / Specialist colour p.156 / File formats p.160 / Print finishing p.162

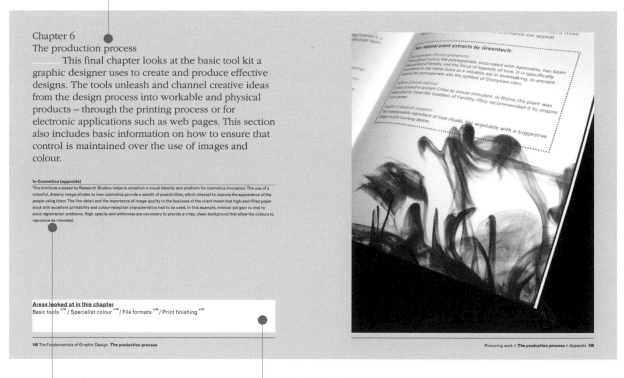

Captions
Each example has a caption to highlight the key points of reference.

Chapter previews
The preview shows the main sub-topics covered by the chapter.

Contagious (right and below)
These spreads from Contagious magazine by Why Not Associates show how design boundaries are constantly challenged. The publication abides by conventions, but is also surprising and engaging. The layered graphic devices and convergence of type and image create a single, unified piece.

CASE STUDY / MCDONALD'S / THE EMPIRE STRIKES BACK / IT'S BEEN A TOUGH START TO THE NEW MILLENNIUM FOR MCDONALDS. THE BURGER BEHEMOTH HAS SEEN ITS STOCK PRICE SLIDE, FACED TUMULT IN THE WORKROOM AND TAKEN FLAK FROM ANALYSTS, OBESITY WARRIORS AND THE ANTI-GLOBALIZATION LOBBY. BUT THE COMPANY IS FIGHTING BACK, WITH HEALTHIER MENU OPTIONS, BOLD INFERIOR DESIGN, A HIP HOP SIGNATURE TUNE, FORTHRIGHT PR STRATEGY AND A RADICAL COMMITMENT TO BRAND JOURNALISM IN PLACE OF TRADITIONAL MARKETING TECHNIQUES.

LUCK ARDEN PRINTED A UK PERSPECTIVE

Westminster Academy (right and below)
Studio Myerscough's design for Westminster Academy in London features environmental graphics in which typography is an integral part of the built environment. In this example, the relationship between the designer and architect, Allford Hall Monaghan Morris, results in bold, engaging and optimistic graphics that clearly inform people of their location.

Built environment
The physical, global construct around us that requires both the colour and interior of buildings.

30 The Fundamentals of Graphic Design: Influences and creative elements

Graphic design: art or craft? < Industrialisation > Technology 31

Graphic design: art or craft? < Industrialisation > Technology 31

Images
Images and designs from contemporary and historic designers are used to explain key points.

Box outs
Box outs provide additional detail about key terms that are underlined in the main body copy.

Identity and branding
——— People tend to use the terms 'identity' and 'branding' interchangeably, but they refer to two different concepts. An identity is the sum of the qualities that are synonymous with the level of service of an organisation. Branding is the process by which this identity is given a visual expression.

Visual identity
The creation of a visual identity seeks to take key behavioural characteristics of an organisation and use them to build an image that can be presented to target consumers, other stakeholders and the world at large. A visual, or branded, identity can take one of three forms: monolithic, endorsed or branded.
  Visual identities present a consistent image that is instantly recognisable and reflects the essence of the organisation. In creating a brand identity, a designer tries to instill meaning and various qualities into the brand or marque by using a combination of colour, typography, imagery and style to evoke a certain feeling in the viewer.
  The interpretation of a design or a reaction to it may change over time and lose immediacy with the target audience. This is one of the reasons why brand logos are periodically redesigned so that they continue to present a fresh and appealing face to the consumer.
  A visual identity goes further than just creating a brand mark, however, and covers every presentation element from colour schemes to typographic structures.

Monolithic identities
A monolithic identity is one where all products produced by a company feature the brand. This is the umbrella logo that is used by all subsidiary companies on all products.

Endorsed identities
An endorsed identity is one where each product has a separate and unique brand, but the brand also identifies the parent company.

Branded identities
This is a fully branded product in its own right and does not include a specific reference to the parent company. In this case, products are identified by separate and unique brands and it may not be obvious who the owner or parent company is.

The Crafts Council
The programme covers featured here were created by INTRO for The Crafts Council. The new brand identity was part of a refresh for the organisation. The heritage and recognition of the old 'C' logotype was maintained and modernised in the rebrand by replacing the original fine-serif font with a bespoke, contemporary type style, optimised for clarity and legibility. The logo is used in a clear position to ensure coherence across a range of publications. It was implemented across a range of media, including stationery, marketing materials, catalogues, signage and website.

These programmes prominently feature the new C Crafts Council logo while the main image relates to a different aspect of craft.

Marque
An icon traditionally used for car branding but now used more extensively as a general brand term.
Refresh
Updating a brand to modernise it and give it a fresh look while maintaining its essential qualities.
Rebrand
Redefining the brand identity of a product, service or organisation to alter its message a.

46 The Fundamentals of Graphic Design Influences and creative elements

Consumerism < Identity and branding > Social responsibility 47

Detailed texts
The texts discuss the topic in hand and why it is important.

Navigation
Chapter navigation helps to determine what section you are in and what the preceding and following sections are.

Introduction

⎯⎯⎯ This book is about graphic design rather than being a book of graphic design. The distinction may seem slight, but it is fundamental to this volume as it covers the graphic design industry and its processes rather than simply functioning as a coffee-table book. However, this book also contains works from highly imaginative creatives, which are used to illustrate the fundamental principles and working methods that graphic designers employ in their day-to-day activities.

Pure Design Classics poster (above)

This poster by Parent Design promotes an avant-garde furniture supplier. It uses a strong grid and is printed on bible paper.

Transport and Water Management (above)

Pictured is a folder created by Faydherbe / De Vringer for the Transport and Water Management Inspectorate following the addition of new divisions, which contains postcards with panoramic views from the archives of the Dutch Photo Museum by photographer Frits Rotgans, a pioneer in this field. Each photo is used to represent a division and the folder was a present for employees and their families.

Graphic design is a broad discipline that encompasses many different aspects and elements. It can be difficult to explain as a fractured discipline because designers work in varied environments and may rarely, or never, engage in some aspects of the practice.

However, as a creative pursuit, there will always be a reason to engage in other areas of the discipline. This book attempts to look at some of these areas and provide a useful resource for designers, irrespective of the particular field in which they work.

Chapter 1
Graphic design as a discipline

Graphic design takes ideas, concepts, text and images and presents them in a visually engaging form through print, electronic or other media. It imposes an order and structure to the content in order to facilitate and ease the communication process, while optimising the likelihood that the message will be received and understood by the target audience. A designer achieves this goal through the conscious manipulation of elements; a design may be philosophical, aesthetic, sensory, emotional or political in nature.

Think! (opposite)

This poster was designed by Leo Burnett for the Think! Copycat Parents' Campaign for the UK Department of Transport. The work highlights the importance of parents setting a good example for their children and is an example of design's power to change people's behaviour and make them question their actions. The message is presented in a child's handwriting and the adult world is represented through the use of printed text. The child's world is represented by the copying of the message in an uncertain hand in various bright colours.

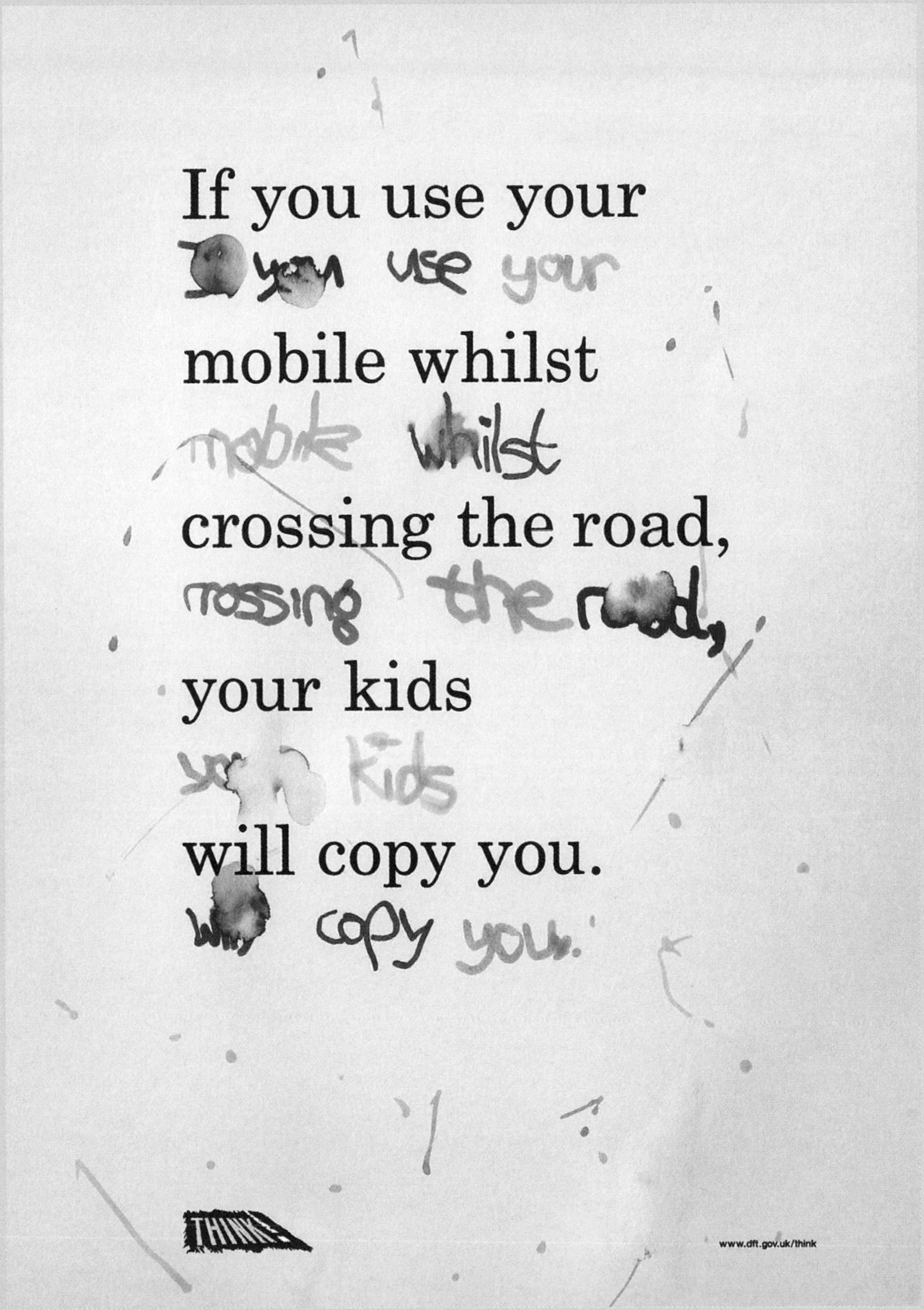

If you use your
mobile whilst
crossing the road,
your kids
will copy you.

THINK!

www.dft.gov.uk/think

What is graphic design?

———— Graphic design is a creative visual arts discipline that encompasses many areas. It may include art direction, typography, page layout, information technology and other creative aspects. This variety means that there is a fragmented landscape for design practice within which designers may specialise and focus.

The evolution of graphic design

Graphic design developed from the printing and publishing industry, with the term itself first used in the 1950s. At that time there was a clear demarcation within the different stages of the print production process, with specialist professionals or trades performing each one. These stages involved printers, scanners, photographic reproduction, graphic design, typesetters, print buyers, film, proofreaders and production managers.

The consumer economy that emerged in the western world following the Second World War brought with it the emergence of bright and attractive packaging as competition between products intensified. The number of magazines also began to increase, resulting in greater demand for visually appealing designs. These coincided with developments in print technology and opened up new production possibilities that designers were well placed to take advantage of. The success of graphic design helped to make it even more indispensable.

As the power of colourful visual communication became widely appreciated, graphic design grew from the need to provide visual communication to the consumer world and spread throughout different sectors of the economy, while continuing to harness the technological developments that progress brought forth.

Technological development, particularly in the digital age, has revolutionised and rationalised the processes of print production. Trades such as typesetting and artwork preparation have become obsolete, as they can now be performed by a designer. As a consequence, graphic design has developed into a multifunctional role that sees the designer playing a pivotal role in the production process. This demands great versatility and the need to communicate effectively with many different professionals. In the past, designers would have undertaken all aspects of a job from the generation of ideas to hand-drawing type for headings and layout.

Technological development has placed designers at the heart of the creative process. Often, a graphic designer manages the design process and coordinates the work undertaken by other creative disciplines as part of a job. As such, the scope of a designer's responsibilities now includes print buying, website programming, photography, page layout, materials selection, art direction, freehand illustration, computer-generated illustration (CGI), project management, client account management, storyboarding, editing and pre-press production.

Monza 1948 (below left)

Max Huber designed this poster to advertise motor racing at Monza, Italy in 1948. It incorporates various elements, such as typography, imagery and colour, to present the concept of motor racing. Although no car is pictured, the design captures the essence of speed and competition through the use of coloured arrows and angled, diminishing type.

Revolutions (below right)

Pictured is a poster created by 3 Deep Design that has similarities to the adjacent Monza poster, made in the pre-computer age, despite the fact that they were created using different technology. Both feature type and images that tell a message and create visual impact. Technology may alter how designs are created and produced, but good design always goes beyond this via the effective application of design principles.

What is a graphic designer?

———— Thinking of graphic design as a trade is anachronistic and limited. It is more useful to look at the underlying approach to design that a graphic designer takes in order to understand his or her role in the print and digital production process. A designer essentially has two roles in the process: satisfying the design brief and executing the job.

Fulfilling the brief

The first task a graphic designer fulfils is to work out what has to be done in order to satisfy a design brief (see page 74). This may involve conducting research into the subject matter in order to generate preliminary ideas. Any project begins as a series of preliminary sketches, thoughts or ideas.

A graphic designer brings a sense of order to these concepts and arranges them in a way that gives them pace and meaning. In essence, a designer creatively structures and edits the job, and makes decisions regarding what is vital to communicate and how best to convey the message.

Executing the job

The designer's next task is to execute the job. Designers may work with, and choose from, a varied selection of sources to conceive the final design – whether employing a philosophical viewpoint, such as modernism, or relying on pure aesthetics, such as current trends in typeface design or fashion.

A valuable part of the design process is the final resolve, look and feel (<u>aesthetic</u> qualities) of the project. Aesthetic control is more far-reaching than selecting sizes and colours as it brings order to a project, and aids communication and understanding. The implementation of a clear hierarchy can both enrich and simplify a project by making it easier for the user to locate and obtain information – whether the job is a complex signage system or a simple restaurant menu.

Aesthetics
Of or concerning the appreciation of beauty or good taste.

Deconstruction
A method of critical enquiry that examines how meaning is constructed by challenging prescribed values which are presented to us. For example, why should folio numbers be small and in the corner of a page?

For Reading Out Loud

This spread is from *For Reading Out Loud*, a collection of poems by Mayakovsky (1893–1930). It was designed by the constructivist El Lissitzky (1890–1941) and published in Berlin in 1923. The role of the graphic designer involves interpreting a brief and producing a design using skills that blur the boundaries between artist, designer, typographer and philosopher.

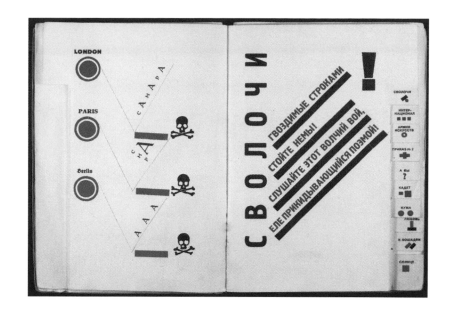

Communicating and conveying messages

A designer can arrange text and images in an infinite number of ways, but the ultimate aim is to communicate effectively rather than produce avant-garde work for its own sake. Design actively develops, maintains and evolves conventions, axioms and clichés in order to convey important messages. For instance, why does the front page of a newspaper contain 500 words and one large picture, a masthead and a standfirst? Because this format has become the convention accepted by readers and anything drastically different may prevent them from buying or reading a newspaper.

Conventions save designers from having to start from scratch with every job. However, this is not to say that there is no room for innovation. On the contrary, innovation tends to occur within the bounds of established convention. Design conventions are a useful and necessary element of society. For example, motorway signs function according to conventions as they communicate messages that can be instantly processed by motorists. If signs did not communicate effectively, there would be more accidents.

On the other hand, the <u>deconstruction</u> method of critical enquiry examines how meaning is constructed by challenging the prescribed values presented to us. The term 'deconstruction' was coined by French philosopher Jacques Derrida in the 1960s to describe a viewpoint that looks at how meaning is constructed. By challenging or deconstructing accepted values, meaning can be delivered in different ways. For example, why should folio numbers be small and located at the corner of a page? Why can't they be large and in the centre of a page?

Group structures and working methods
———— A designer can fulfil various roles in different environments and company structures. They can be involved in many different activities and work with a host of other creative professionals. Each design studio has its own particular ethos, style, goals, influences and culture. The following pages outline some of the environments a designer can work within.

Design groups

A designer's main route into design practice and gaining practical experience is to obtain an internship at a design studio after completing art college. When choosing which studios to apply to it is worth considering aspects such as size, areas of expertise and creative thrust. For example, a large design group may have more staff, bigger offices and higher overheads than a smaller studio, which will impact on the type of work they undertake. A large agency may be too expensive for smaller companies to commission, while a smaller agency may not be able to handle the demands of a large account.

Clients tend to look for design studios of sufficient size, experience, skill and reputation to match their needs. On top of creative skills and credentials, administrative support and workflow management also need to be considered as a mismatch may cause severe problems.

Designers tend to have a feel for the type of company they are comfortable working for. Some are drawn to big-brand clients involved in many different sectors that are serviced by bigger design agencies. Others are drawn to smaller bespoke projects where there may be more creative freedom. It is important to research your choices well so that you stand a better chance of matching your needs to those of a prospective employer.

Internship

An opportunity for a student to acquire practical work experience and the chance to apply the material learned in an educational establishment. Internships typically take place during academic breaks.

Faydherbe / De Vringer

This stationery created
by Faydherbe / De Vringer
makes use of two distinct
colours to reflect the fact that
the two individuals work
closely together within
the company, but have
distinct personalities.

Local, national and international design groups

The dominance of a design group in a particular region has a significance that goes beyond the floor space and number of employees it has. A small agency in a provincial town will usually – although not always – have a very different client list and undertake different design activities from an international design group. Both types of agencies have strengths and limitations. A local design group with its finger on the pulse of local culture can provide a focused service that is in tune with current trends. However, such an agency may not be equipped to deliver an international solution, not due to lack of creative talent, but because of structural reasons, such as not having the scale to manage a big project. An agency with experience in many geographical areas would be better suited to this type of job.

Some design groups have offices in several countries to serve international clients, but still have to remain targeted and focused in each of their locations.

For example, Research Studios, founded by Neville Brody and FWA Richards in 1994, has offices in Paris, London and Berlin. Designers in each of their branches have local knowledge that combine with the pooled resources, knowledge and administrative strengths of an international company.

Another example is Pentagram, a studio originally founded by Alan Fletcher, Colin Forbes and Bob Gill. Pentagram has offices in London, New York, San Francisco, Austin and Berlin, and each office offers a team of partners with particular design specialisations that can be pooled when necessary. Having a group of experienced designers in each location offers a multinational client company a sense of security that a smaller company may not be able to provide. Ironically, multinational clients may at times seek avant-garde design solutions and require maverick individuals or smaller design studios to provide them.

Office size and work relationships

An office contains a complex series of relationships between the different staff members and management; there are different levels of control, authority, freedom and formality independent of the size of the firm. Large agencies can provide a range of experience on large international projects, but as they employ many people, a designer may only get to participate in a limited range of activities. However, large design agencies are likely to have the capability to work on a range of different projects in different media.

Working in a smaller studio may provide a designer greater opportunity to work with the lead designer or partner. This could mean more involvement in the creative aspects and tasks within design projects and the design process. However, smaller agencies may specialise in serving particular market segments or in working with specific media, which may restrict the breadth of work a designer undertakes.

It is important to match your aspirations with the type of organisation that can provide your needs in order to obtain personal and job satisfaction.

Hierarchies

Different design agencies have different structures that range from the informal to a formal hierarchy extending from the owner or manager, through to head designers, art directors and the designers. Other agencies prefer team-based structures that include a writer, designer and programmer; some operate more like a collective to encourage greater fluidity, while others use a team of designers surrounded by support staff, such as project managers working with several designers.

Ground Zero viewing wall (above)

The temporary installation created by Pentagram for The Port Authority of New York and New Jersey comprises information panels at the memorial site of the former World Trade Center. The wall is a grid of galvanised steel that allows visitors to witness the site redevelopment. The names of those who died in the 2001 attacks are listed in the recessed bays.

Account handlers and project managers
An account handler has a direct relationship with both the client and the designer. The account handler receives and helps to define the design brief, liaises with the client, instructs the design team and presents the design to the client. This structure allows the design team to focus on responding to the brief while the account handler deals with the administrative aspects of the project and client relations. A lack of contact between the client and design team can result in a poor communication of requirements if the account handler is not a good communicator.

Project managers work with both the client and design team to ensure that a project progresses to budget, schedule and brief. In addition, project managers help to source copy, images and organise photo shoots. A client typically talks to the head designer about the design and the project manager about costs. This division means there is potential for a communication breakdown when decisions are made without all parties being present. For example, a designer and client's decision to use a special printing technique will have cost implications that the project manager needs to know about. Excellent communication skills are crucial – without them, creative work cannot be effectively facilitated.

Account handler structure

Client

Account handler

Design team

Project manager structure

Client

Design team

Project manager

These hierarchical structures can be found in many large design groups, but they are applicable to small companies and studios as well.

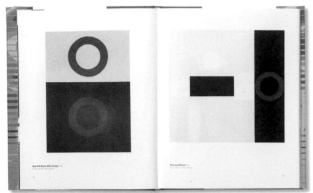

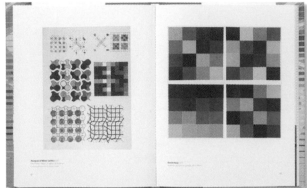

Ways of working

Many designers prefer the freedom and responsibility of working in smaller organisations either as a freelance, sole trader or part of a partnership, which perhaps allows them to specialise in particular design solutions. Working within a smaller entity generally allows a designer to have greater creative freedom and to be constantly involved in the 'big picture', including working closely with the client. Small-scale design organisations often become well-known for having a particular design style, a specialisation in serving certain sectors or in working with certain materials.

Freelancers

A freelancer is self-employed and hired on a job-by-job basis by an agency or company. The term originated from the Middle Ages when knights without allegiance to any given lord were effectively deemed a 'lance for hire' or 'free lance'. Within graphic design, a freelancer may have a specific skill that is required in a given project, such as Flash animation. At times, they are generalist designers who prefer to work with greater autonomy and freedom, relishing the challenge and diverse opportunities of working for a variety of clients.

Freelance work can be culturally and financially rewarding, although it requires dedication, organisation and the need to constantly develop and maintain a client base to ensure a continuous flow of work. This often depends on maintaining excellent service levels and a good professional reputation. Registering with creative agencies for ad hoc jobs is also helpful.

Michael Kidner

This book was created by father and son partnership, Webb & Webb. The small structure of the design studio allows the partners to have direct client access and total control over the creative and project management processes. This reduces the possibility for miscommunication and allows the team to find optimum solutions to client briefs.

Sole trader

Sole traders generate their own work rather than performing work on an ad hoc or informal basis for another design agency. Some designers follow this route and rent desk space in a shared studio with other designers or creatives to benefit from a sense of camaraderie. Freelance life can be a lonely experience due to solitary working conditions or spending short periods of time in a company where one is a stranger. Often, sole traders will commission freelancers as their workload increases; they register as a limited company to obtain additional benefits as their business expands.

A limited company is a separate legal entity from the people who own it and has the advantage that its debts are separated from its owners. However, official accountancy procedures that are legally binding must be adhered to and the directors of the company have legal duties to comply with. Companies pay corporation tax rather than income tax, and this can be an efficient way for a designer to handle tax issues. This will depend on the size and scope of the business.

Partnerships and collectives

A sole trader may later enter into a partnership or collective with like-minded individuals or those who can bring a different skill set to the team. This is typical of a collective that forms to benefit from a cross-fertilisation of ideas and talents. This embraces the 1960s idea of the commune where people come together for a specific project and then separate. This is a fluid working structure, but it is difficult to keep together due to its informality.

Working with other people requires a high level of trust and understanding between group members for personal, financial and legal reasons. For clarity and the protection of all parties, the entity should be established on a legal basis to clearly indicate who has responsibility for what and how finances, debts, profits and ownership are decided. Another option is to go for a limited liability partnership. This has the benefit of limited liability whilst maintaining a traditional partnership.

Graphic design today

——— Graphic design has evolved and adapted to change by incorporating new technologies in communicating to an ever more segmented audience. It poses a number of questions: Where does this process of evolution leave graphic design today? What is the currency of modern graphic design? What does graphic design seek to do?

Text and image

Text and image are the mainstays of graphic design and their arrangement on a page, screen or in the built environment is one of the ways through which people communicate in the modern world. Numerous groups compete for our time and attention; our attention spans are getting shorter, which means messages need to be abbreviated. Designs have to work harder and on different levels in order to communicate effectively. Different design elements must complement each other in order to enhance the overall communication.

Storytelling

Designers are modern storytellers who try to make sense of the world through the arrangement and presentation of text and images. Narrative development is one of the issues mentioned throughout this book and is one of the essential elements that a designer instils within a publication. A narrative is constructed by using text and image to create meanings, which can be achieved in many ways through the use of symbolism, metaphor or other devices.

Questions to ask when constructing a narrative:

General		Specific to example (opposite page)
What:	*What are you trying to say?*	*Report on the financial performance of a company*
Why:	*Why is your message unique?*	*Presenting it in a way that makes the information accessible and interesting*
Who:	*Who is the message for?*	*For shareholders, regulators, customers, staff and other stakeholders*
How:	*How are you going to do it?*	*Through juxtaposed, contrasting metaphorical images*
Where:	*Where will the message appear?*	*In the annual report*
When:	*When will it be delivered?*	*In 2007, reporting on the 2006 financial year*

Wienerberger annual report

This annual report by Austrian firm Büro X exemplifies one of the main challenges faced by modern graphic design: namely, making that which is difficult to understand understandable, and that which is uninteresting, engaging. The designs in this report are honest, straightforward and engaging in spite of its heavy subject matter. The piece recognises that brick production is not necessarily very stimulating, even if it is a profitable business. The design uses specially commissioned photography and a lenticular cover to provide colourful and juxtaposed, contrasting images that are relevant to the company and its staff members.

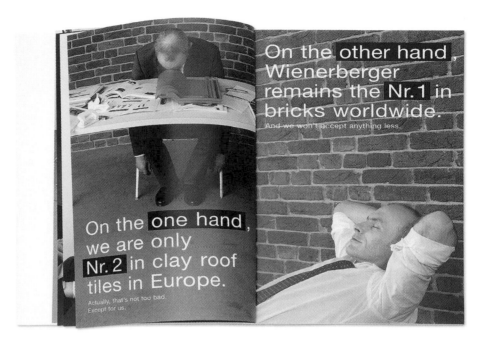

Chapter 2
Influences and creative elements

Graphic design is subject to the evolving intellectual and aesthetic trends that influence the work of designers and reflect the attitudes of society at large.

For example, design responds to the changing themes that govern the way we view the world and this is evident in movements such as Modernism, Postmodernism and Deconstructivism. These trends help shape the development and evolution of graphic design as a creative discipline, opening new doors of creative possibility and providing new tools with which to meet design challenges.

Bird

These spreads from the book *Bird* were created by 3 Deep Design. They are an example of a craft-based approach to typography and image-making that is not constrained by technology. The design exhibits a high level of artistic freedom and personal expression through the use of sewn images, type and detailing in different coloured thread and hand-painted images. The images in these spreads were drawn by Kat Macleod.

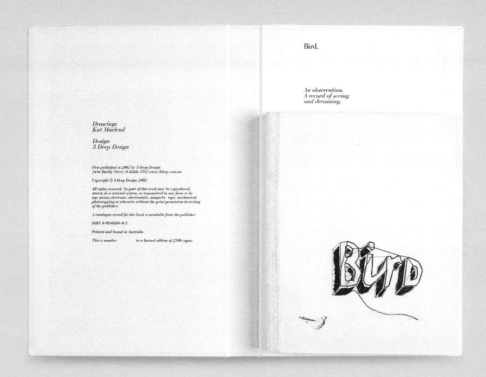

Graphic design: art or craft?

———— Graphic design is a multidisciplinary process that draws on many creative sources. Some view it as a craft – one of the trades of the traditional printing and publishing process – while others see it more as an art. This subtle distinction can be of fundamental importance to a design, as will be seen in the following sections.

Design as craft

As a craft, graphic design is an integral part of the print production process that involves preparing text, image and other content for publication. As such, a graphic designer occupies a key role in the process by liaising with the client and other professionals such as printers, typographers, photographers and finishing houses. This view of graphic design as part of the print process sees graphic design as a craft.

Some elements of design work, such as the addition or subtraction of space between letters to create well-typeset and attractive text, can be considered as a designer crafting the type in a similar way that a carpenter works a piece of wood or a letterpress printer adjusts the bed pressure to create the correct type impression on the stock. This view sees the designer as having a relationship with a client as part of a commissioned process, with the designer facilitating what needs to be done to produce the job.

Design as art

As an art, graphic design creates striking images and layouts to communicate ideas and information to different audiences. The discipline is at the forefront of creative thought, advancing theory on how to communicate effectively through visual media by using a wide range of intellectual tools to establish meaningful connections between different design elements. This view of design sees the designer as a separate entity who is preoccupied with personal expression rather than being led by a brief or a commission.

Many designers undertake personal experimentation projects and produce self-published work whereby their intentions can be closely linked to those of an artist. However, the two views on design are not mutually exclusive. Many designers are commissioned for their unique styles, while other designers adapt their style to suit a specific commission.

Reappropriation

Taking elements from mainstream culture and re-inserting them into peripheral culture or vice versa.

London's Largest Living Room (above)

London's Largest Living Room was created by Gerrard O'Carroll for the London Architecture Biennial and Design for London. The installation is a combination of art and craft as the designers turned their hands to a variety of disciplines to produce the final result, a return to the multidisciplinary practices of the Renaissance period. The detail shows the carpet design that was 30m x 14.5m and produced using 500mm square tiles upon which the living room was arranged and laid out. The carpet was designed by Studio Myerscough.

Blanka (above)

This Paul Barruel illustration was commissioned by NB: Studio and features the <u>reappropriation</u> of a traditional style as part of a contemporary look. The black-and-white image is styled like an engraved plate, such as those that were traditionally used to illustrate books; it is shown here to illustrate the fact that graphic design draws from many disciplines. An engraved illustration is one that would have been carefully crafted to present an accurate impression of the subject, yet it is intrinsically beautiful and can stand alone as a work of art. The design process, by commissioning pieces, often blurs the line between whether something is considered as art or craft.

Industrialisation

———— Industrialisation in the eighteenth century saw the mechanisation of the printing industry, which allowed for higher print runs and greater production rates. More importantly, it brought dramatic changes to the print and production processes as type and typesetting methods changed to support faster production rates.

Printing developments

New and faster printing presses presented new demands on other elements in the printing process, such as the type used to print, the stock printed on and the way whole pages were prepared for print.

Printing press

The printing press underwent dramatic changes following the Industrial Revolution. Wood was replaced by cast iron, which resulted in increased printing pressure and a greater print area.

Friedrich Koenig created a steam press that by 1814 could produce over 1,000 impressions an hour, as well as doubled-sided printing. In 1833, the rotary press was invented by Richard Hoe, which meant millions of copies of a page could be printed in a single day. The subsequent development of rolls or webs of paper resulted in mass production.

Line casting

Machines such as the Linotype enabled type to be set at much higher speeds. An operator entered text on a keyboard and the machine would arrange moulds or matrices for the text into a line, which were then cast as a single piece or 'slug' – literally a line of type. This invention revolutionised newspaper publishing.

Photoengraving

Photoengraving replaced the use of handmade printing plates with a photochemical process that engraved a metal plate using photographic techniques. An acid-resistant, photosensitive material is applied to a metal plate bearing the design to be printed. Exposure of the metal to acid dissolves the exposed metal, engraving the image on to it. A similar process is used to make intaglio – printing plates that have depressions for the ink to sit in.

Intaglio

A printing technique using an image from a recessed design, which is incised or etched into the surface of a plate. Ink lies recessed below the surface of the plate, transfers to the stock under pressure and stands in relief on the stock.

Industrialisation led to great changes in how print was produced. The items pictured here show how printing evolved over time: (left to right) a page printed in early Latin, incunabula, dated 1483; a letterpress alphabet that became common during the Industrial Revolution; and a newspaper printed by letterpress (Columbian Centinel of Boston, published 06 May, 1809).

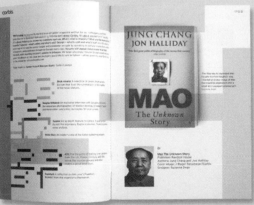

Corbis (above and right)

This *Volume* magazine was designed by Jog Design for the image library, Corbis. It features typography reflecting the pixelated structure of digital type. The digital age has supplanted the industrial age and most publications are now designed and set electronically using pixels rather than picas.

Contagious (right and below)

These spreads from *Contagious* magazine by Why Not Associates show how design boundaries are constantly challenged. The publication abides by conventions, but is also surprising and engaging. The layered graphic devices and convergence of type and image create a single, unified piece.

THE EMPIRE STRIKES BACK

80/61

CASE STUDY / McDONALD'S / THE EMPIRE STRIKES BACK / IT'S BEEN A TOUGH START TO THE NEW MILLENNIUM FOR McDONALD'S. THE BURGER BEHEMOTH HAS SEEN ITS STOCK PRICE SLIDE, FACED TUMULT IN THE BOARDROOM AND TAKEN FLAK FROM ANALYSTS, OBESITY WARRIORS AND THE ANTI-GLOBALIZATION LOBBY. BUT THE COMPANY IS FIGHTING BACK, WITH HEALTHIER MENU OPTIONS, BOLD INTERIOR DESIGN, A HIP HOP SIGNATURE TUNE, FORTHRIGHT PR STRATEGY AND A RADICAL COMMITMENT TO 'BRAND JOURNALISM' IN PLACE OF TRADITIONAL MARKETING TECHNIQUES.

LUCY AITKEN PROVIDES A UK PERSPECTIVE

Westminster Academy
(right and below)

Studio Myerscough's design for Westminster Academy in London features environmental graphics in which typography is an integral part of the <u>built environment</u>. In this example, the relationship between the designer and architect, Allford Hall Monaghan Morris, results in bold, engaging and optimistic graphics that clearly inform people of their location.

Technology

——— Graphic design, like many other disciplines, is linked to technology at many different levels. Technology affects how designs are produced and it also influences developments in style, art and society as a whole, which in turn are reflected in the form a design takes. Technology also offers designers a variety of media outlets for their projects.

Graphic design and technology

It would be easy to think of graphic design as a discipline that is solely influenced by artistic or academic concerns. However, it is also shaped by advances in technology, which bring new considerations and processes for a designer to utilise and manipulate. Design principles are highly transportable and transferrable through different technological epochs, which are modified and refined along the way.

Technology has democratised design by simplifying production processes and extending access to the tools used to generate designs. Digitisation has revolutionised design so that it can be mass reproduced utilising ever more diverse delivery systems, such as wireless hand-held devices and diverse online mechanisms, as information delivery migrates away from print media.

Technology not only affects the delivery mechanism, but also the design. Images and text can be subject to far greater manipulation and intervention at quicker speeds than in the past. This poses the threat that design may become a form of urban noise where the message is lost and diluted among the plethora of other messages that bombard society.

Advancements in technology open up new avenues of creativity by putting new tools into the hands of the designer or allowing designers to produce work more rapidly. This in turn provides more time for experimentation and can provoke profound changes in the design process. This is evident in how the Apple Macintosh (1984) allowed designers to escape the limitations of the paste-up board.

Newspapers have been pioneers in the application of new design technology, such as four-colour printing and the use of the Internet. Consumption culture readily adapts to the benefits of technology, this means that traditional media also face a threat from technological developments such as digital media.

Whether technology is a threat or an opportunity depends upon one's perspective and ability to adapt and change. For example, newspaper print subscriptions may be falling, but online subscribers are increasing, allowing newspapers to provide other services to readers.

Kunstenplan Vergezichten.
Het woonzorgcentrum De Leemgaarde
in Westvoorne is sinds een tijd vier
kunstwerken rijker. In opdracht van
provincie Zuid Holland werd door
kunstgebouw een kunstenplan voor
De Leemgaarde geschreven getiteld
Vergezichten

Kunstenplan Vergezichten (above)

Faydherbe / De Vringer's pixelated digital
image shows what is possible due to
technology and the digital revolution.
Technological development continues to
provide designers with new tools and
techniques for creation, but the need to
harness the tools available to good effect
remains constant.

Bacardi Limón (above)

New York agency, Vault 49, designed this poster by utilising the capabilities of digital
technology. The design evokes a sense of fun and retains a simplicity that is
reminiscent of illustrated advertising art from the early twentieth century. Although
its creation was made possible by technology, the imagery is not technology-led.
Vault 49 could have produced a similar job by using a different method, such as
hand illustration.

Fuse

These posters are from digital
typography magazine *Fuse*. 'Lush us',
created by Jeffery Keedy for Fuse 04
(Exuberance) and F Trojan, created
by Simon Staines for Fuse 12
(Propaganda), are examples of the
creative possibilities that the
digitisation of typefaces has unlocked.

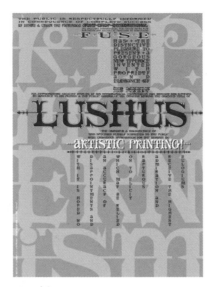

Digitisation of typefaces

The use of photocomposition in the 1970s accelerated the type production process as characters could be projected from the screen of a cathode ray tube on to light-sensitive paper or film, which could then be stored in a magnetic memory, overwritten and edited. This period also saw the introduction of dot matrix and digital typography.

The introduction of personal computers in the 1980s broadened font development opportunities, allowing for characters to be drawn and amended quickly, while type shapes could be easily copied to form the basis of different letters. The acceptance and use of digital type was assisted by the development of PostScript – the standard used for digital typesetting in the late 1980s. However, this is now being superceded by the Portable Document Format (PDF).

Open Type

Open Type – a scalable format for computer fonts developed by Microsoft and joined by Adobe in the 1990s – is now the dominant standard for digital font production. It can support up to 65,536 glyphs in a font and has advanced typographic features. Digitisation has reduced the cost of type to the extent that it has changed from being an expensive specialist tool to a commodity product, which now poses a stern challenge to type foundries.

It is estimated that there are now over 100,000 digital fonts available – there may be a lot of choice but as a result, decision-making is made more difficult.

Subsequent improvements in technology have increased the speed and power of personal computers, reducing the time needed to create new fonts, many of which have been showcased in the typography magazine *Fuse* – launched in 1991 by Jon Wozencroft and Neville Brody.

Sample font

Sample typeface

a b c d e

Typefaces and fonts

The words 'typeface' and 'font' are commonly used synonymously although they possess distinct meanings. There is usually no harm in this as the substitution is quite universal.

The distinction between typefaces and fonts is arguably more important now that the two seem to occupy the same space.

A typeface is a combination of characters, letters, numbers, symbols, punctuation and other marks that share a similar design. A font was traditionally something physical, such as lithographic film or metal type characters (pictured above).

Digital type foundries

Digital technology has led to the development of digital type foundries, organisations and companies that use computer software to produce type in electronic format rather than the cast metal symbols that characterised printing from the Industrial Revolution until the 1980s. Digital type foundries, such as Emigre, FontFont and Jeremy Tankard, harness the benefits of digital technology to produce a wide range of fonts, exploring and developing the form of text characters. Digital production has seen an explosion of the number of typefaces available due to the relative ease, speed and low cost of producing and storing them compared to traditional type creation techniques.

the quick brown fox jumped over the lazy dog

Negative tracking (above)

the quick brown fox jumped over the lazy dog

Negative leading (above)

A number set from a font of metal type characters.

The examples above show the effects of negative tracking and negative leading, both made possible by digital typography.

The impact of digital typefaces

In the digital age, fonts are no longer just physical objects. This means that a designer has more options available regarding font usage, which offer more opportunities for control and manipulation, for example, in terms of leading and spacing.

The image above shows a block of numerals in metal type, which were used for printing text before the advent of digitised type. As these are physical items, it was not possible to overlap type or have negative leading, something that is now taken for granted in the use of computer-generated type.

Tracking and leading

Type spacing can be altered on both the horizontal and vertical planes by manipulating tracking and leading – two processes that have become more flexible with digital typefaces.

Tracking works on the horizontal plane; it is the amount of space that exists between the letters of words, which can be adjusted to bring characters closer together or take them farther apart. Tracking can be reduced to condense space between letters or removed completely with negative tracking. On the other hand, increased tracking adds space, which can prevent characters from touching each other. More specific adjustments can be made in the space between two letters by kerning (removal of space) or letterspacing (addition of space).

Leading works on the vertical plane and refers to the space between the lines in a text block. The term originates from the strips of lead placed between the rows of metal type letters to keep constant space alignment – a function digital leading still serves. However, digital type also allows for negative leading, resulting in overlapping or the absence of space between text lines.

glyph switching avoids visible character repetition

fonts designed specifically for screen

The Beowolf typeface was created by Erik van Blokland and Just van Rossum in 1990 – an example of 'glyph switching'.

Verdana is a sans serif font specifically designed for screen use. It is easy to read and is compatible with different operating systems.

Glyph switching (flipping)

Glyph switching or flipping is where a digital typeface contains multiple versions of characters, enabling a design to create an eclectic look within the limitations of a single character set. Flipping is an example of technology presented in a certain way so as to appear non-technological by including random differences that add a touch of the accidental, such as the random printed marks produced by the wear patterns of letterpress characters. Commands in the PostScript code refer to a random generator that makes the character outlines irregular.

The use of glyph switching makes a design look as though it was not produced using current technology when technology is actually facilitating it. There is a certain irony in the fact that the designers of digital fonts are trying to achieve a non-uniform effect, while printers using traditional technology strive to overcome quirks and irregularities in their finish.

Fonts for screen

Fonts are now designed specifically for use with digital applications such as the Internet. Fonts designed for screen use are created so that they can be used on a wide range of different systems while giving the same performance. The existence of web-safe fonts means website producers can increase the likelihood that the content will be displayed as required.

Microsoft produced a standard family of fonts for Web use. Of these, the following are web-safe fonts: Arial, Courier New, Georgia, Times New Roman, Verdana, Trebuchet MS and Lucida Sans.

With only a limited range of web-safe fonts available, it is probable that a company may not be able to use its font choices in all arenas. This means the fonts for its offline communications may be different to those used for its online communications.

Other limitations of web-safe fonts when used in print applications is that the serifs can be too fine – the fonts can be overly broad and they can fill in with ink when printed.

Typography

—— Typography is the means by which a written idea is given a visual form. It is one of the most influential elements that establishes the character and emotional attributes of a design; the visual form it takes dramatically affects the accessibility of an idea and how a reader reacts towards it.

Variety and creativity

Typefaces vary from clearly distinguishable letterforms that flow easily before the eye, to more elaborate and eye-catching forms and vernacular characters appropriated from the urban environment. The different styles and forms of fonts enable them to communicate in ways that go beyond the words they spell out; different typefaces can be said to have different personalities, and it is these personalities that a designer often focuses on when selecting fonts for a particular job.

Typography is a discipline that continues to evolve as computer technology makes the process of font creation quicker and easier, as well as more experimental. In addition to appropriating elements from the vernacular, typography is also self-referential – the origins of many of the fonts in current use can be traced to designs created during earlier historical epochs, from the earliest days of printing to Roman tomb inscriptions. Designers can harness this heritage to instil their designs with historical references.

This section will look at many different examples of typographic design and how type is used to communicate. It will also look at how fonts are classified into different families and systems that help to organise and better understand the many thousands that exist. The ability to classify typefaces is essential to design and effective communication – different fonts have different characteristics, histories and personalities.

Typeface classification is based on the anatomical characteristics of the letters and are generally categorised as: block, roman, gothic, script or graphic, with several further sub-classifications. Typeface classification loosely charts the development of fonts over time and gives an indication of the historical development of type.

Audi (right)

This 1970s Audi Fox poster by Helmut Krone features an avant-garde, sans serif typeface. The design has clear references to the design discipline itself – the visual reference borrows from the pangram 'the quick brown fox jumped over the lazy dog'. Pangrams are used to showcase typefaces as they are holo-alphabetic – they contain every letter of the alphabet at least once. The poster says as much about the typeface as it does about the car.

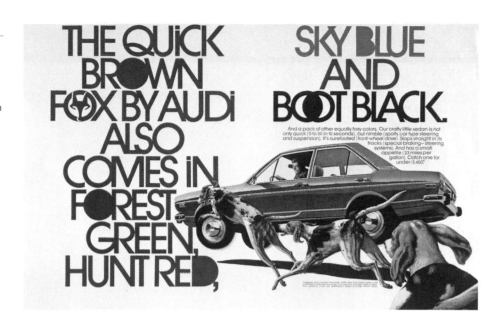

Space (below)

Derwent London's twice-yearly publication is designed by Studio Myerscough. It features both nostalgic and contemporary typography and borrows from previous times and reappropriates the styles to create a modern approach that is engaging and dynamic. Note how the letterforms of the title overprint.

Slam (below)

This book cover by Studio Output feature eclectic and colourful type that jumps out at the reader. This dramatic impression is created by the use of large-format, orange type set against a black background and fine, white-line art illustrations.

Bonfire (above)

Research Studio's advertisement for the Bonfire Snowboarding Company features a simple yet clear type hierarchy that imparts information about the people modelling the clothes: the person's name, what they do and what they wear. Brand information takes a secondary role. The models are real people photographed by famous snowboard photographers and the type reflects solid authenticity with its filled-in counters.

Big Lottery Fund (below)

These typographic A2 posters were created by The Team for an internal brand for the Big Lottery Fund, following its formation from the merger of the New Opportunities Fund and the Community Fund. The key messages of teamwork (circle), service excellence (star), accountability (plus sign) and valuing people (tick) were screen printed in a single colour to give a simple yet memorable message.

Teamwork
One of BIG's internal values

Service excellence
One of BIG's internal values

Accountability
One of BIG's internal values

Valuing people
One of BIG's internal values

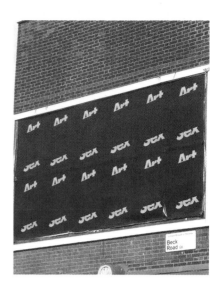

Seduced (above)

These printed pieces by Research Studios use type to form strong visual shapes that are still readable in spite of parts of some characters being cut away. The way the words 'art' and 'sex' have been partially covered suggests both voyeurism and censorship, which are relevant concepts to the subject of the exhibition.

Moving card (right)

A thermographic ink was used to print this card. It has an expanded number five depicting the company's new location: 5 Park Place. Thermography is a print-finishing process used to produce raised lettering on paper substrates by depositing a powder on the printed piece while still wet; it is then passed through an oven. In this example, the numeral has been expanded as much as possible, while still remaining legible and recognisable. This project was created by Parent Design.

Park Place
Poole

Type classification

The wide range of typefaces available means that a way of classifying them is essential, particularly to simplify the communication of specifications for a piece of work. Typefaces and families of type can be classified according to the inherent characteristics of their anatomical parts.

Roman

Roman
The basic cut of a typeface is the roman version, so-called due to the inscriptions found on Roman monuments. Roman is sometimes referred to as 'book', although this can be a lighter version of the roman face.

Italic

Italic
A true italic is a drawn typeface based around an angled axis. These are normally designed for serif typefaces. Obliques are slanted versions of sans serif typefaces rather than newly drawn versions.

Condensed

Condensed
Condensed types are narrower than the roman cut and are useful when space is limited.

Extended

Extended
Extended types are wider versions of the roman type. They are often used for items such as headlines to dramatically fill a space.

Boldface

Boldface
Bold, boldface, medium, semi-bold, black, super or poster – all refer to a typeface with a wider stroke than the roman cut.

Light or Thin

Light or Thin
Light is a thinner version of the roman cut.

Blackletter
Typefaces based on the ornate writing style prevalent during the Middle Ages. Also known as Block, Gothic, Old English, Black and Broken. The typeface shown is Goudy Text.

Old style
Roman fonts that have a slight stroke contrast and an oblique stress. This font group includes Venetians and Garaldes. The above type is Garamond.

Italic
Based on Italian handwriting from the Renaissance period where letterforms are condensed. Originally a separate type category, they were later developed to accompany roman forms. The type shown is Garamond italic.

Script
Fonts that attempt to reproduce engraved calligraphic forms. This type is Kuenstler Script.

Transitional
Transitional typefaces marked a divergence from Old Style forms towards modern forms at the end of the seventeenth century. It is characterised by increased stroke contrast and greater vertical stress in curved letters. The font shown is Baskerville.

Modern
Typefaces from the mid-eighteenth century typified by extreme stroke contrast and the widespread use of hairlines and unbracketed serifs. The type above is Bodoni.

Square serif
Typefaces that have little stroke weight variation and thick, square serifs – as shown by the Clarendon type above.

Sans serif
Typefaces without serifs and little stroke weight variation first introduced by William Caslon in 1816. The type shown above is Gill Sans.

Serif / sans serif
A recent development which encompasses typefaces that include both serif and sans serif alphabets. The above type is Rotis.

Consumerism

——— The demand for a wider range of goods results in fierce competition between manufacturers and like products. Consumerism impacts on graphic design because product packaging and advertisements have an increasingly narrow and restricted window of opportunity to connect with the consumer.

Taking account

The concept of branding has developed with the rise of consumerism as marketeers have seen that people tend to respond to something familiar when faced with a multitude of different visual stimuli. Marketeers hope that their brand, and its accompanying logo, will be the familiar face in the crowd that grabs a consumer's attention.

In order to succeed in this highly competitive environment, products and services are designed to provide character and individuality, and to instil sales appeal. This means that the designs representing the face of a product are becoming increasingly sophisticated, which can result in a clash between the aesthetic principles of a designer and the taste of the general public or target audience. This can pose the philosophical question of whether it is a designer's job to give the public what it wants or what they do not know they need. Cigarette packaging is an interesting example in this context as designers are faced with the challenge of creating an alluring design that complies with the legal requirements to include highly visible health warnings.

Personal choices

Ultimately, the type of client you are willing or unwilling to work for is a question of personal choice. For some, the thought of working on an alcohol or tobacco product is unthinkable, while others draw no distinction between these and other products.

For many designers, this may not be a clear-cut decision and some product types or companies may fall into a grey area. For example, a designer may not be willing to design a new cigarette carton for a tobacco company, but would create leaflets warning of the health risk involved in using the product for the same company.

Adbusters

Canadian anti-consumerism magazine, *Adbusters,* seeks to challenge the role of the graphic designer in the erosion of our physical and cultural environments by commercial forces. The magazine frequently appropriates and reworks the messages of well-known, global brands to present what it sees as the true story behind them.

Action and reaction

The graphic design industry includes many people who collectively and individually are responsible for creating the images and communications used to boost consumerism. Many designers are protagonists in the backlash against what is seen as rampant consumerism, which began in the UK in the 1960s with the publication of Ken Garland's *First Things First* manifesto (1964). This was supported by over 400 graphic designers and artists who sought to re-radicalise design, emphasising that design is not a neutral, value-free process. Many graphic designers now actively participate in <u>culture jamming</u> – the subverting of well-known corporate symbols and messages – to reflect other perspectives that people have of the global, corporate consumer world.

Anti-consumerism

While graphic design played a key part in the rise of consumerism, it is also used as a tool against it. *Adbusters*, through its 'Buy Nothing Day' does not ask the public to abandon its consumerist activity, but to question it. The misery of choice has never been more apt than in graphic design today as there are more modes of communication, more products, more people to sell to and more fonts to choose from; but do any of these ultimately make us happier? Designers can make a difference to consumer culture by thinking about the design industry's contribution to this phenomenon and completing jobs in a non-exploitative manner, in a socially, economically and environmentally sensitive way at no cost of others.

Culture jamming

Culture jamming uses existing mass-media messages and twist them so that they provide pithy comment on themselves. The *Adbusters* magazine is a well-known example of culture jamming and it seeks to draw attention to the practices of global corporations that are contrary to the often idyllic images and messages they produce in order to reinforce and promote their brands. Culture jamming engages in various campaigns, such as 'Buy Nothing Day', 'TV Turnoff' and 'True Cost Economics', that seek to challenge consumerism and the consumer's role in society.

Identity and branding

———— People tend to use the terms 'identity' and 'branding' interchangeably, but they refer to two different concepts. An identity is the sum of the qualities that are synonymous with the level of service of an organisation. Branding is the process by which this identity is given a visual expression.

Visual identity

The creation of a visual identity seeks to take key behavioural characteristics of an organisation and use them to build an image that can be presented to target consumers, other stakeholders and the world at large. A visual, or branded, identity can take one of three forms: monolithic, endorsed or branded.

Visual identities present a consistent image that is instantly recognisable and reflects the essence of the organisation. In creating a brand identity, a designer tries to instil meaning and various qualities into the brand or marque by using a combination of colour, typography, imagery and style to evoke a certain feeling in the viewer.

The interpretation of a design or a reaction to it may change over time and lose immediacy with the target audience. This is one of the reasons why brand logos are periodically redesigned so that they continue to present a fresh and appealing face to the consumer.

A visual identity goes further than just creating a brand mark, however, and covers every presentation element from colour schemes to typographic structures.

Monolithic identities

A monolithic identity is one where all products produced by a company feature the brand. This is the umbrella logo that is used by all subsidiary companies on all products.

Endorsed identities

An endorsed identity is one where each product has a separate and unique brand, but the brand also identifies the parent company.

Branded identities

This is a fully branded product in its own right and does not include a specific reference to the parent company. In this case, products are identified by separate and unique brands and it may not be obvious who the owner or parent company is.

The Crafts Council

The programme covers featured here were created by INTRO for The Crafts Council. The new brand identity was part of a refresh for the organisation. The heritage and recognition of the old 'C' logotype was maintained and modernised in the rebrand by replacing the original fine-serif font with a bespoke, contemporary type style, optimised for clarity and legibility. The logo is used in a clear position to ensure coherence across a range of publications. It was implemented across a range of media, including stationery, marketing materials, catalogues, signage and website.

These programmes prominently feature the new C Crafts Council logo while the main image relates to a different aspect of craft.

Marque
An icon traditionally used for car branding but now used more extensively as a general brand term.
Refresh
Updating a brand to modernise it and give it a fresh look while maintaining its essential qualities.
Rebrand
Redefining the brand identity of a product, service or organisation to alter its message.

Shine (right and below)

Studio Output presents PR company Shine by employing an antithesis. Instead of being shiny, the identity is cool and understated, but has an exciting and vibrant flash of colour. The identity features consistency in the restricted colour palette. It has the same typeface throughout and focuses on aspects such as the circle motif present on different pieces. This consistency is essential to ensure that the brand appears in the same way regardless of the media or production methods used. The designer must therefore ensure that the design is flexible and adaptable. This is easier to achieve when the design is kept simple.

Non-visual identity – values

An identity seeks to combine those attributes of an organisation that are considered important and central to its success in a way that appeals to the target audience. An identity is successful when selected attributes capture the essence of the organisation well. These need to be communicated to the target audience in a way that is credible and well-executed. A successful identity creates a strong impression about the values and function of an organisation.

Glacis Beisi (below)

This design by Büro X features the manifestation of a brand. The reservation card uses the same typography as the brand and the napkin holder features the company logo.

BKK Architects (below)

The project below is part of a visual identity created by 3 Deep Design for BKK Architects. It uses monotone patterns to create a strong, memorable presentation with designs that suggest construction and the interplay of light.

MVS (right)

Parent Design's colour-coded stationery for audio and visual supplier MVS features a simple narrative that relates to, and explains, the activities of the company.

Pattern (below and below right)

This identity for fabric design group Pattern demonstrates a clear influence from the sector in which the client operates. The images show scenes from the studio and the use of the identity in situ. Pattern's identity usually appears on hangers (bottom left) and it relates to the texture and detail of the fabrics. The identity was created by Mark Design, London.

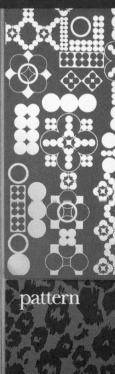

Flores (right)

The brand developed by Studio Output for Flores restaurant had items that were meant to be public-facing, so consistency across the different items, such as menu cards, was essential. The image shows how a floral-based brand mark is used to instantly identify the restaurant on all the items. Notice how the process of identification is aided by the consistent positioning of the brand mark in the lower right-hand corner of each piece. The floral nature of the restaurant's name inspires the graphics and natural colour scheme used.

Branding

Branding is a process that allows a company to differentiate itself and its products from its competitors, while also establishing positive links to its customers in order to create and preserve loyalty. Branding is important in competitive markets as it provides a means for consumers to make buying decisions based on their perceptions of the brand; this may include quality, safety, luxury, value or other considerations that are important to the consumer at the moment of purchase.

Brands initially developed as a way of identifying livestock and cattle. However, from the moment Andrew Pears produced the Pears transparent soap in 1789, brands have been used by manufacturers as a way to make their products stand out from the rest of the competition.

As the use of brands became more widespread, companies saw that certain consumers exhibited loyalty to particular brands. Companies then sought to create brands representing desirable qualities because consumers were beginning to buy brands rather than products.

Some brands, such as Starbucks, Adidas and Coca-Cola, have grown globally and send the message that a consumer can obtain the same product bearing the same qualities anywhere in the world. The rise of global brands has also spurred the development of niche brands that differentiate themselves by being personal rather than ubiquitous.

Branding is now a major consideration in the design of public-facing items that the general population can access. For example, the 'Pattern' identity featured on the opposite page presents a uniform face to the public, which also represents the values and characteristics of the organisation.

Brand development

Some brands or identities are stand-alone designs created for specific applications, while others need to be designed with the flexibility to work in different applications and environments, having bolt-on or sister brands, such as the example logo below. These bolt-ons are sometimes pre-planned, but often have to be developed at a later date as a company expands into new markets.

One Housing Group (below)
This logo was designed by Blast for One Housing Group. It uses an 'O' to represent a sense of oneness, uniformity and unity. This logo is versatile and can be used with various logotypes to represent different areas of the business and group.

Group subsidiaries

Group businesses

 Community Action   CityStyle Living Ltd   CHA Ventures Ltd

Plymouth Arts Centre
(right and below)

This dynamic and vibrant identity was created by Thirteen for Plymouth Arts Centre in the UK as part of a brand development brief. The brand identity is robust enough to be used over a range of different stationery items and other printed pieces due to the consistent use of the coloured line treatment. The result is a striking brand image obtained through the use of vibrant lines. Notice how some of these are printed while others are produced by a die-cut that shows colour through from the stock underneath.

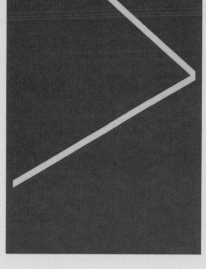

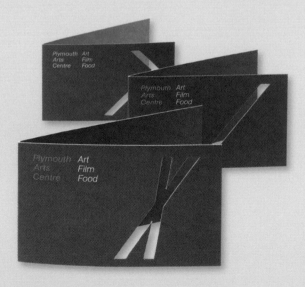

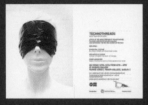

**Technothreads
(above and right)**

This identity was created
by Studio Myerscough
for Technothreads and
uses an image of a bound
mannequin as the basis for
the visual identity and brand.
This example shows that an
identity can be created by a
distinctive image or attitude
rather than a traditional
logo. This identity appeals
to the savvy target audience,
and adds credibility and
authenticity as well as
arresting the viewer with
a memorable and striking
brand.

Brand guidelines

Companies spend a lot of time and money to develop their brands, but their manifestation, or how they will appear in the public domain, may be dealt with by several entities in different countries. In order to exercise control over how various people will implement the use of a brand, companies also develop brand usage guidelines so that the company identity is effectively represented as intended. Brand guidelines are a clear set of instructions on how to use a brand, and equally importantly, how not to use it.

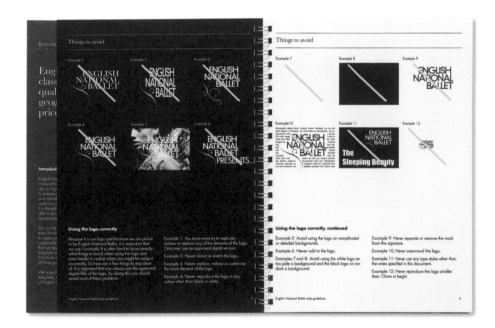

**English National Ballet
(left and below)**

Pictured are brand guidelines designed by The Team for the English National Ballet as part of a brief to create a campaign to restore the passion for the English ballet. The brand proposition aims to break down the barriers between the audience and the dancers by painting an intimate portrait of the dancers behind the scenes and capturing the moment of anticipation before they enter the stage. As with other brand guidelines, it includes detail on how to use the brand and its imagery. Guidelines often include handy tips and notes for a designer who is using the brand in a project – for example, recommending a minimum measurement for the space where the logo is to sit.

Social responsibility

———— Within the design industry there is a trend to question ethical standpoint in relation to worldwide issues such as gender, poverty and global warming. Organisations increasingly foster and promote their own ethical positions to guide their activities, which can result in conflict with personal ethics.

Agency vs designer standpoint

The ethical position of a design agency, a designer and a client should all come to light during the interview stage, as all parties seek to establish whether there is a good fit among them.

Ethics may cause problems when a design agency accepts a commission for a company or product that a designer is ethically opposed to, such as work on alcohol, cigarette or animal fur brands. As the anti-consumer lobby grows, designers often find themselves caught between the two sides as their job involves making products look more appealing. More and more designers question their involvement in promoting products or services that they deem ethically or morally questionable.

Designers have a key role to play in creating the visual fabric of the world around us and are instrumental in producing the cultural tapestry that binds us together as a society. This ultimately comes with responsibility for the outcomes of design.

Charity vs paid work

There is the perception that work performed for charities is donated or undertaken for free. This is not always the case as charities, like any other business, realise that they get what they pay for. Most large, successful charities are run as businesses, and they procure design in the same way as any other firm. For a charity to operate successfully, it needs to use design as a tool to convey the very specific messages that it thinks are important in order to stir people and create the social leverage they require to effect change.

While some agencies may choose to work for reduced fees (or even for free) for charities or causes they support, such work is rarely free. Payment could take other forms and may not always be tangible. Agencies can receive positive publicity that extends to a wider population, cultural kudos for supporting specific values and, in some cases, they may have greater creative freedom than with corporate clients. However, this could also close the door to working with companies that the charity may be targeting.

Recycled paper

Recycled papers are those produced using 100 per cent recovered fibre, which may be pre- or post-consumer, such as waste paper.

Vegetable inks

Ink made from linseed and soya vegetable oils that have been developed to replace oil-based printing inks, which are less toxic and easier to remove than traditional pigment transfer vehicles. This eases de-inking during the paper recycling processes.

DANDELION & RED CLOVER TEA

Therapeutic herb blend of burdock, dandelion, red clover, sage and cleavers

MADE IN ENGLAND
50g | 1.76 oz

Neal's Yard Remedies (left)

This tea packaging was produced using recycled paper and vegetable inks to provide many benefits. The unbleached paper is stronger than bleached paper, which means that less packaging is required, weight is reduced and transportation costs are lowered. The cellophane window is made from eucalyptus rather than plastic.

We will change a broken world (below)

NB: Studio's poster for the charity Christian Aid features a simple, yet stark, graphic that aims to jolt people and raise awareness.

Individual responsibility

As individuals we consciously and unconsciously attempt to influence the moral behaviour of others. As a designer, this may come in the form of encouraging clients to use less packaging; issuing smaller format publications; using recycled paper instead of heavily filled art paper; sending HTML emails rather than a printed material version; or reducing the number of overs allowed for in the print run, which may eventually end up in a landfill site.

One school of thought believes that fewer, but higher-quality products should be produced so that people will keep them for longer in order to move away from the disposable culture that our society has readily adopted. Junk mail or bulk mail is considered a nuisance by an increasing proportion of the population, and it may only be a matter of time before designers and the studios they work for are unwilling to contribute to this communication channel that generates a huge amount of waste.

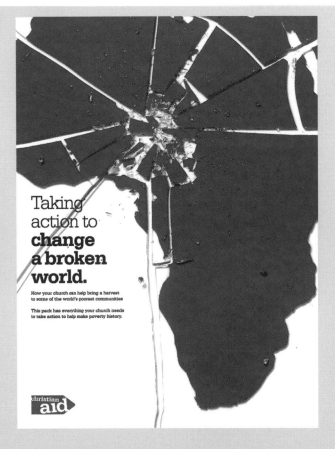

Taking action to **change a broken world.**

How your church can help bring a harvest to some of the world's poorest communities

This pack has everything your church needs to take action to help make poverty history.

christian aid

Modernism and postmodernism

———— Modernism and postmodernism refer to two different views of the world that developed and guided creative activity at different points in the twentieth century. Modernist and postmodernist thinking still have relevance today and their influences can be seen in contemporary designs as people seek to make sense of the world around them.

Modernism

Modernism through the cubist, surrealist and Dadaist movements was shaped by the industrialisation and urbanisation of western society. Modernists, including the De Stijl, Constructivism and Bauhaus movements, departed from the rural and provincial zeitgeist prevalent in the Victorian era, rejecting its values and styles in favour of <u>cosmopolitanism.</u> Functionality and progress, expressed through the maxim of 'form follows function', became key concerns in the attempt to move beyond the external physical representation of reality through experimentation in a struggle to define what should be considered 'modern'.

In graphic design, modernism embraced an asymmetrical approach to layout with strict adherence to the grid, an emphasis on white space and sans serif typography, and the absence of decoration and embellishment.

Postmodernism

Postmodernism (1960–present) is a creative movement that emerged following the Second World War and questioned the very notion that there is a reliable reality. Postmodernists deconstructed authority and the established order by engaging in the ideas of fragmentation, incoherence and the plain ridiculous.

A reaction to the sometimes bleak and impersonal Modernist movement, postmodernism returned to earlier ideas of adornment and decoration, celebrating expression and personal intuition rather than formula and structure. Postmodernism continues to be the dominant force in creative thinking where the preference is for complexity, contradiction, diversity and ambiguity rather than the rational order and simplicity that characterised modernism.

Cosmopolitan

Having an exciting and glamorous character associated with travel and a mixture of cultures.

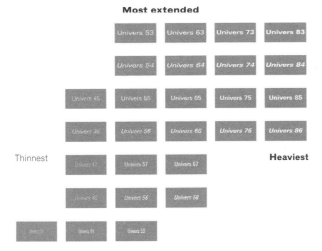

Most extended

Univers 53	Univers 63	Univers 73	Univers 83
Univers 54	Univers 64	Univers 74	Univers 84
Univers 45	Univers 55	Univers 65	Univers 75	Univers 85
Univers 46	Univers 56	Univers 66	Univers 76	Univers 86
Univers 47	Univers 57	Univers 67		
Univers 48	Univers 58	Univers 68		
Univers 49	Univers 59	Univers 50		

Thinnest — Heaviest

Most condensed

Frutiger's grid showing the relationship between type weights.

Olicana – a font that mimics handwriting.

Modernist fonts

The quintessential philosophical differences between modernism and postmodernism are never more apparent than in font and typeface design. Modernism saw the rise of cleaner, simpler sans serif fonts, which turned their back on elaborate serif fonts and brought a sense of order to typography. This saw the use of consistent stroke weights and rounded forms to give evenly weighted characters, such as Helevetica Neue.

A new sense of order was brought to typography by the modernist numbering system developed by Adrian Frutiger to easily express the relationship between the different weights and widths of his Univers typeface. In this system (shown above), the first digit in the font's name represents the weight of the font from three (light) to eight (heavy), while the second digit relates to the width from three (extended) to nine (condensed). Frutiger's grid gives designers an easy-to-use matrix of fonts that allows for rapid selection of type styles for different aspects of a design, which helps to ensure compatibility.

Postmodernism and typeface design

Postmodern fonts have moved away from the clean-cut and well-organised forms of modernist fonts and have returned to embrace more elaborate and decorative forms, which include the return of the serif and uneven stroke weights. Postmodernist fonts celebrate ornamentation and personal expression, and also look to include the randomness that is present in handwritten and letterpress printed texts.

Handwriting

The Olicana font is an example of a font that mimics handwriting (see above). In order to more closely provide a facsimile of handwritten text, this font has multiple glyphs available, which means that repeated characters are not always the same. It also includes an occasional ink blot, thumbprint or smudge to add to the impression that the text was written with a fountain pen. Obviously, there is no need for a font to mimic handwriting when type is set on a computer, but this font works well and is a very convincing approximation of handwriting.

Arts and Crafts

This spread from a book designed by Webb & Webb features text and images that were placed and organised on the page according to a grid. Notice how this creates clean sight lines as the images and text align with each other and the margins.

The grid

The grid is a template or guide used for positioning and organising the elements of a design in order to facilitate and ease decision-making. Grids are the bone structure of a layout and serve as a tool to help a designer achieve balance while presenting a potentially large degree of creative possibilities.

The use of grids, fields and matrices allows a designer to take a considered approach to design, which makes effective use of time and space. It also ensures that different design elements work together to provide consistency and coherency throughout a body of related work.

Since humankind first began recording information there has been a need to organise content. The page structures that are commonly used today can be traced back to Classical times. Theories on proportions and the division of space developed in Ancient Greece.

The grid, as a containment structure for visual communication, has evolved in tandem with developments in mark-making technology, becoming increasingly sophisticated as handwritten manuscripts were replaced by early printing, movable type, linotype and computer-to-plate printing.

The grid serves to establish parameters to guide the placement of text and elements, but strict adherence to such guidelines can be restrictive. Leading designers often challenge the structure and confines that a grid provides in order to provide the best possible solution to the design brief.

There are many types of grids, including those with many columns, those with few, and those comprising of fields or modules rather than vertical columns. Two of the main grid types are shown on the opposite page.

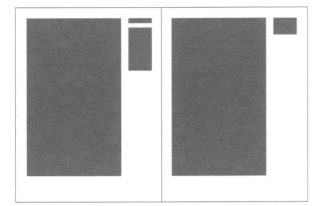

An asymmetrical grid has pages on the spread that look exactly the same.

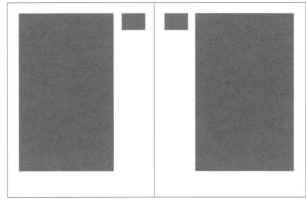

A symmetrical grid has pages on a spread that mirror each other.

The asymmetrical grid

An asymmetrical grid is one where both pages in a spread use the same grid, which means one page is a copy of the other. These grids may have a bias towards one side of the page (usually the left), created by having one column narrower than the others. This provides an opportunity for the creative treatment of certain page elements while retaining overall design consistency. The narrower column may be used for captions, notes, icons or other elements, and in this way, it is often treated as a wide margin for outsized marginalia.

An asymmetrical grid tends to create a sense of movement from the left to the right due to the way the eye first fixes on the large column before moving to the thinner column for both pages of a spread.

The symmetrical grid

With a symmetrical grid, the verso page is a mirror image of the recto page. This gives equal inner margins and two equal outer margins to a spread. To accommodate marginalia, the outer margins are proportionally larger than the inner margins. This is a classic layout pioneered by typographer Jan Tschichold (1902–1974) based on a page size with proportions of 2:3. The simplicity of the layout and pages creates spatial relationships that hold the text block in harmonious proportions. This grid projects harmony because it is created using relative proportions rather than absolute measurements.

A symmetrical grid tends to be calmer to read than an asymmetrical grid as both pages cause the eye to look inward towards the spine, creating a calm and balanced space for the reader rather than a sense of movement.

Architecture and the 'Special Relationship' (above)

These spreads by Gavin Ambrose for Taylor and Francis/Routledge illustrate how a grid needs to relate to the contents of a publication. Here, the use of a simple grid allows for the effective placement of images and text. Tension is introduced in the design by offsetting the images and having them cross the centrefold. However, the absence of full bleeds results in the images being constantly framed, bringing an element of consistency to the design.

Rationel (below)

Mark Design, London's product guide for Rationel Windows leaves the grid visible, making it an obvious and integral part of the design. The grid frames inset images that alternate between detailed and scenic shots. While the grid is rigid, pace and variation are added through the use of different image configurations.

The various elements of a grid:

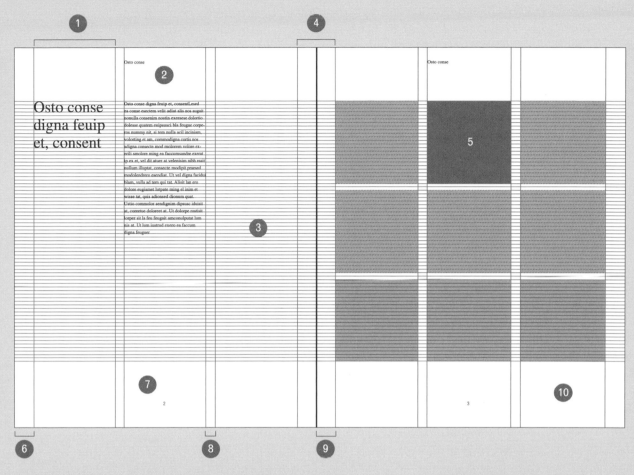

1 Column
The basic structure for organising body text. Text generally flows from one column to the next, left to right.

2 Top margin
Space at the top of the page that sets the boundary of the design. Sometimes contains running heads, chapters heads and folios.

3 Baseline
The imaginary lines upon which text, images and other graphic elements are set.

4 Centrefold
The centre of a spread where the pages are fixed together with a binding.

5 Picture box
A space for pictures and other image elements.

6 Outer margin
The space at the edge of a spread.

7 Bottom margin
The space at the bottom of a page that usually has folios.

8 Inter-column space (also called gutter)
The space between two text columns.

9 Gutter
The inner margins at the centre of a spread located on either side of the binding.

10 Text block
The main body text of the publication that runs in columns.

Nostalgia and rhetoric

——— Designers use various methods to convey meaning, often tapping into shared cultural norms, values, history and language. The use of symbols or heroic figures from the past to support or represent a viewpoint or certain qualities is an example of the use of nostalgia and rhetoric.

Nostalgia

Nostalgia is the longing for past situations, bringing a feeling that things were better then than they are today. People derive comfort from the familiar and designers use nostalgia to create, transfer and instil positive associations from the past into a design or product of today. For example, advertisements for Hovis bread employ nostalgia through images of a small baker on a cobbled street to instil the values of tradition, quality and small-town reliability into a product that is mass-produced under factory conditions.

As consumers, we often seek robust traditional values, yet we expect the cleanliness and convenience that the modern world provides.

Rhetoric

Rhetoric is the art of using language effectively in order to persuade an audience. It originates from the Greek *rhetor* meaning 'the art of the orator'. The ability to speak or communicate well by using language precisely, clearly and in a way that is readily accessible to the audience may at times be more important to winning an argument than the facts under discussion.

By keeping in mind the persuasive nature of rhetoric, designers can structure designs and control the presentation of information so that it bears more weight, impact and the element of trustworthiness. How information is presented can be more persuasive than the bare facts.

Values
Sets of collected beliefs held by an individual or social group in which there is an emotional investment. Values differ widely from person to person and group to group, and can lead to acrimonious divisions when they conflict.

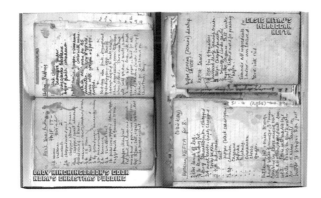

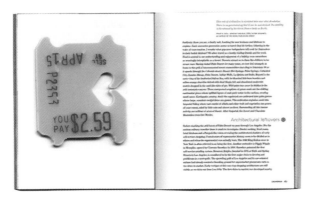

A Tale of 12 Kitchens

A Tale of 12 Kitchens is a cookbook written, photographed, designed and typeset by Jake Tilson. The author's eclectic style draws on the nostalgia and rhetoric of his everyday life. His design brings an entirely new vision to food – its context, the way it is grown, packaged, bought and cooked – and evokes powerful memories and emotions. For example, the illustration of the Marmite jar is a clear nostalgic reference to childhood, as is the image of the plastic bread-bag tag. The book is also interspersed with comments in a large typesize, which act as section breaks.

Semiotics

——— Semiotics is the study of signs that offers an explanation of how people extract meaning from words, sounds and pictures. An understanding of semiotics helps a designer to instil work with references that enable them to communicate multiple layers of information to a reader.

Semiotic principles

Designers use images to communicate. When images are developed through the application of semiotic principles, a graphic device can be made to mean more than it would appear to be at first glance. The type of image, its style and presentation, its quality and how it has been reproduced can all add layers of meaning to the overall design, drawing different meanings from the context in which it is placed. The bee design (opposite) for Waitrose honey is a good example of this as three parallel lines on the bee's body become an 'E' within the context of the row of letters they are placed in.

Sign

Signs are often graphic elements that are used to visually represent an object, person or idea by reducing it to simple and instantly recognisable characteristics. For example, through the sign or signifier 'dog', an image of a dog is conveyed; the letters 'd', 'o' and 'g'; or a recording of a bark, give the same message. A dog can also be represented by a graphic sign, sketch or icon. An example is the red cross – a widely recognised sign indicating that people can obtain medical treatment.

Symbols, icons and indexes

Symbols are physically recognisable representations of items, while icons rely on a shared understanding. For example, 'dog' could also be a symbol – a pictorial element that communicates a concept, idea or object, such as a sign, pictogram or a graphic element, which describes an action, or series of actions, through visual references or clues. A red cross is a universally understood icon, which means help or medical treatment.

Indexes are signs that link to an object – for example, a horseshoe or an anvil could be an index for a horse.

Symbols

This horse image visually represents a horse because it looks like a horse.

Icons

This horseshoe icon represents a horse at its most basic level, but it implies other meanings such as horse racing and even luck.

Indexes

This anvil is a link or index to a horse or blacksmith, although it depicts neither.

Waitrose honey packaging

Turner Duckworth's packaging for Waitrose honey features a simple typographic treatment that plays with the 'E' in 'HONEY' to create an icon in the form of the stripy body of a bee. The versatile design is also an index because it suggests a slotted wooden honey spoon.

Made in Medway (right)

Made in Medway is a book designed and produced by Steve Rowland in collaboration with Medway Renaissance, an organisation that champions the Medway region of the UK. The book features works and insights into artists and designers in the area. On a denotative level, the title type clearly conveys what the book is about. On a cognitive level, the use of type that has been threaded implies craft or being handmade.

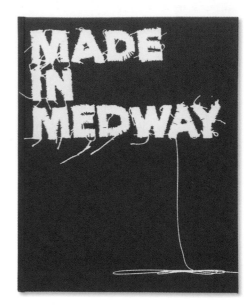

Cognitive

The way in which an image is presented dramatically affects how information is interpreted. Images are powerful communication devices because people can extract many different values from them as they often have cognitive meanings far beyond their denotative elements.

Cognition refers to things that we have perceived, learned or reasoned. A picture of a woman denotes a female, but woman may have other connotations such as family, beauty and love. In the example above, the visual presentation provides cognitive hooks that colour how we interpret the information presented, both in terms of the vivid red colour and the font selection.

Denotative

A denotative meaning is the explicit literal meaning that we take from an image, essentially, taking what we see at its face value. For example, 'woman' could mean or indicate someone of the female gender, or be a mother or sister.

Graphic designers need to consider both the cognitive and denotative values that may be instilled into a piece of work due to the way that information is presented. Different and possible interpretations can lead to confusion and contradiction where there is conflict between what we see (denotative) and what we perceive (cognition).

  B B B

Font choices

Fonts are not just symbols representing sounds; they also have cognitive qualities that help tell stories, which means designers need to consider things that are conveyed in addition to what is actually said. For example, each of these six fonts has a different personality that says more than just 'B' to a reader.

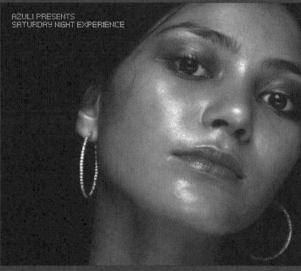

Saturday Night Experience (above)

Pictured here are CD covers created by Mark Design, London for the Saturday Night
Experience music compilations released by Azuli Records. The images are close-up
portraits that have a lot of light reflection appearing like perspiration on the faces of
people. They project a cognitive meaning of clubbers and dancers, while the black
background suggests or denotes the late night, after-club experience.

Vernacular

———— The everyday language through which a group, community or region communicates is its vernacular. It is a recurrent aspect within graphic design as designers draw on the vernacular by incorporating 'found' items, such as street signs and borrowing low-culture forms of communication, such as slang.

Found items

Designers are collectors of images, colours, textures, letterforms and other visual stimuli. They are cultural scavengers and the appropriation of elements are accidentally or unexpectedly found in their work.

For example, the visual language of illustration and typography, whether from a 1970s airline safety card or the signage of an old tobacconist, has a history and style that serves as a source of inspiration.

Placement

The placement or relocation of found items is important, as putting an item within a new time and context can change its meaning significantly. The typography from the signage of an old tobacconist would carry a different meaning if it were placed on the signage for a modern tobacconist or the cover of a music CD. When using vernacular as a design tool, a designer needs to be aware of the connotations it will carry. When an item is used out of context, the work may acquire new meanings that convey wit or irony, some of which may not be intended or recognised until later.

Appropriation

When a designer takes the style used in a design and applies it to another, often in a very different context to the original. This may be done for several reasons: to incorporate the same graphic devices into a job; to use the visual statements provided by the appropriated style; or to add easily decipherable meaning to a job, such as energy or political overtones.

Irony

When the intended meaning of a word, phrase or design is different from its literal meaning, which typically depends on context and circumstance. The incongruity that irony represents is often used to inject an element of humour into a design, or to highlight a discrepancy. For irony to be effective, it has to be clear to the target audience. Designers use the fact that not everyone will recognise the irony of a particular image or situation as a means of tailoring a message to specific groups of people.

Heal's packaging
These toiletry bottles created by Brandhouse for quality retailer Heal's, appropriate the use of paint swatches on a range of bath oils and accessories. Using the values of the client, Brandhouse created a design to extend its product range into new markets.

Vernacular typography

There are numerous examples of vernacular typography and many modern typefaces are in fact redrawn versions of fonts found by typographers in old books. One of the most famous is the font Template Gothic (shown below) by Barry Decks. It is a typeface based on the signage of a laundrette. Having been appropriated from other sources, vernacular typography can add meaning to a work because it has its own personal history or story to tell, giving it added personality. The typefaces below demonstrate that they are more than simply letterforms – they carry additional meanings that should be considered when selecting fonts.

Vernacular image-making

Images can also make use of vernacular inputs to alter their perceived meanings. Designers draw inspiration from the graphic possibilities and the visual language found in the urban environment. These elements are then often incorporated into their own work. Presenting information in a certain style, such as the graffiti found on any street corner in a city, will incite different reactions from various groups. Teenagers may respond positively to the message presented, while adults may shun it.

Template Gothic

typefaces also tell stories

Academy Engraved

typefaces also tell stories

Chapter 3
The graphic design process

_____ The graphic design process involves all the steps necessary to produce a piece of printed or electronic work – from agreeing a brief with the client to sketching conceptual ideas for design development and liaising with those involved in the production process, such as printers and programmers.

How this process is structured and undertaken is dictated by the complexity of a job, the range of media it is being created for and the number of other people involved in the process.

Working with large clients and agencies may entail more steps than working with smaller organisations, and each job requires a different combination of design skill sets.

Bond Bound (opposite)

Pictured is an example of a creative typography produced by Webb & Webb for a book about the cover art of James Bond books. The Os of the title are used to form the first part of Bond's 007 code name, with a die cut in the second O referring to the roving gun barrel sequence from the titles of all James Bond films.

Areas looked at in this chapter

The brief [p74] / Articulating design [p76] / Sources of inspiration [p78] / Design as problem solving [p80] / Creative thinking [p84] / Wit and humour [p86] / Layers of meaning [p90] / Development and experimentation [p92] / Art direction [p96] / Prototyping [p98] / Commissioning art [p102]

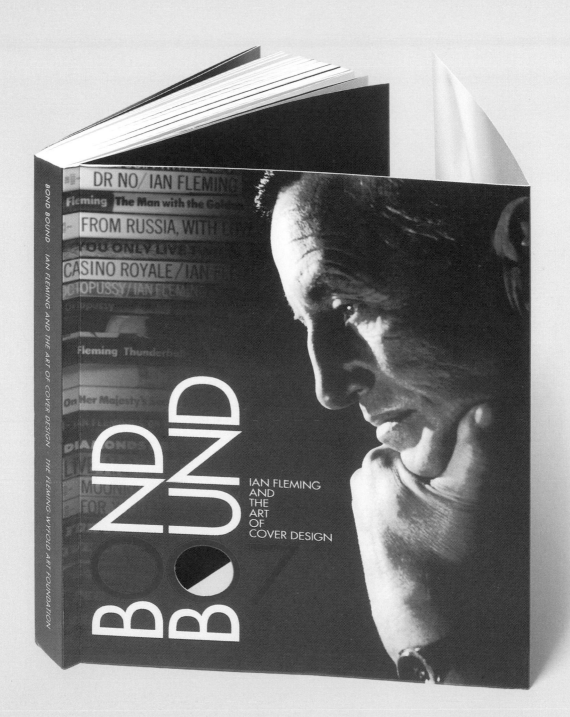

The book cover shows:

BOND BOUND

IAN FLEMING AND THE ART OF COVER DESIGN

Spine text: BOND BOUND   IAN FLEMING AND THE ART OF COVER DESIGN   THE FLEMING-WYFOLD ART FOUNDATION

Background book spines: DR NO / IAN FLEMING · Fleming The Man with the Golden · FROM RUSSIA, WITH LOVE · YOU ONLY LIVE · CASINO ROYALE / IAN FLEMING · OCTOPUSSY / IAN FLEMING · Fleming Thunderball · On Her Majesty's · DIAMONDS · LIVE · MOON · FOR

The brief

_____ The brief is the outline of what a client wants to achieve by commissioning a design. Armed with creative thinking tools, personal influences and source material, a designer can respond to a brief and generate creative solutions for it. However, it must be noted that there are two distinct kinds of brief.

Formal

A formal brief is a written document provided to a designer together with supporting reference material detailing a clear set of objectives that are to be met by the design. These criteria can relate to creative aspirations, aesthetic values, brand development, or more tangible goals, such as redesigning a website to convert more hits into sales. The objective could also be less tangible and harder to measure, such as raising a <u>company's profile</u>.

Whatever the aim, having a formal brief allows all parties involved to understand what is intended. It can be referred to during the project to ensure that it is 'on brief', meaning the design is being produced according to the brief's requirements.

Informal

The second type of brief is informal and is often little more than a fleeting conversation or telephone call. In such instances, it is important for the designer to take notes and ask questions in order to get a clear understanding of what is required and why. It is good practice to follow an informal conversation with a letter or email which can be sent to the client to confirm that there is a shared understanding regarding the brief. This also formalises and solidifies the aims and objectives of the project. This briefing method allows the designer to tap into the enthusiasm of the client, which may spark ideas during the conversation.

Company profile

The public's perception of a company, their products or activities. A company's idea of the public's view of them is not always the same as the public's perception. Therefore, a realigning a company's profile is sometimes necessary.

Rewriting the brief

Designers often rewrite a brief received from a client as doing so allows the design team to ingest the client's requirements and restate them in a way that is more conducive to producing a solution. This may involve a subtle change in language or a more profound rethink of the project's goals. For example, a client may think they need a new website to increase sales, but the better solution may be to develop new marketing material.

A designer's failure to deliver the intended results may be due to a poor, vague or misunderstood brief. Rewriting the brief gives the design team an opportunity to challenge, clarify and realign the brief to ensure that it is clear and that the final design meets the stated goals of the client.

100% Design

This series of posters was created by Blast for the 100% Design show. The brief required a show concept that was less corporate than previous years and more appealing to the potential design exhibitors. In response, Blast produced a strong concept that resulted in an engaging campaign based on the idea that good design improves the environment. Using a subtle play on the conventions of environmental campaigns, the resulting images acted as a call to action for designers to come together to improve the environment. The photographer, Sanjay Kalideen, was briefed to compose dramatic shots that convey the feel of a fashion shoot.

Articulating design

———— A design communicates in many different ways and works on many different levels because it can include a range of concepts and references. Each design element can communicate to an audience, but messages may not be readily identified, acknowledged or understood by all viewers due to differences in how people receive or interpret information.

Design choices

A designer has to select from numerous choices available. As seen previously, typography is not just a bunch of letters and fonts, but elements that are selected with reference to their historical or philosophical origins, and how they look, fill and colour a space. Colours evoke different emotions and bring a host of meanings and references. An image may be a straightforward representation of an object or it may represent something totally different depending upon how it is treated, and the relationships it enjoys with other design elements.

Initially, a client may not make all the connections and interpretations that a designer has instilled into a job. Presenting work often requires a designer to explain the thinking behind the choices made in order for the client to understand its merits. For example, the Nike swoosh and the Starbucks character logo have become incredibly successful designs even though the vast majority of people do not know what they represent or the reasons behind the design choices made.

Subjective / objective viewpoints

Meaning can be given or generated from a subjective or objective point of view and it is important to evaluate both when producing a design. A subjective viewpoint could be what a design means to the target consumer, while everyone else has an objective viewpoint regarding its meaning.

Establishing a desirable subjective viewpoint that appeals to the target audience without alienating other people is not as easy as one might think. For example, what may be a cute bunny rabbit that appeals to one group of people could seem tacky and tired to another.

DEdiCate

Vault 49's design for *DEdiCate*, a Paris-based fashion and lifestyle magazine, blurs the boundaries between graphic design, photography and illustration. This multidisciplinary agency uses various media to produce stunning designs such as the one pictured. Notice how illustration has been used to augment the qualities of the photograph and enhance its visual appeal.

Quantitative / qualitative choices

The motivations and circumstances behind buying behaviour varies greatly and people respond differently to the quantitative and qualitative aspects of information presented. For example, one group may be more interested in the price of a bottle of ketchup, while another makes its buying decision based on the quality of the ingredients. The complexity of an individual's quantitative and qualitative preferences means that they change from product to product. A person who buys ketchup according to its price may buy mayonnaise based on its taste or ingredients. Having an understanding of what considerations are important in the decision-making of a target group allows a designer to incorporate such sought after information triggers into a design.

Micro / macro levels

People have a varying appreciation of scale and perspective, and their awareness of passing through micro and macro levels also varies. Some people readily grasp an over-reaching concept, but get stuck on the details, while others grasp the details well but cannot fathom the bigger picture. A design needs to communicate at the appropriate level so that the target audience can understand the information presented.

A design can be critically appraised for its aesthetic qualities, but while this is a valid practice, a design always generates a response in those who view it, regardless of whether a critic thinks it is good or bad. While years of experience and training stand behind a designer's choices, their approach to a job will not be the same as that of a marketeer, fund manager or client. This may cause conflict, but one must bear in mind that a designer does not design for themselves but to satisfy the needs of a client who may have a better sense of what the ultimate target group will respond to.

Sources of inspiration

——— Design is a discipline shaped by a varied and eclectic set of influences from both the past and present, which inform the choices and decisions made during the design process. Influences may be profound or partial and may influence the overall structure and content of a job, or appear as a subtle twist.

Urban environment

Designers may be influenced by the vernacular language of the urban environment to produce a piece that is current and modern, or work with classical ideas when dealing with spacing and proportion.

Art

Art has always influenced design. The principles that have defined and guided art movements have readily been adapted and brought into design, particularly those relating to page layout and composition. For example, the rule of thirds is used to define the focal point within a piece of work, while the rule of odds is used to make more interesting compositions.

Movies

The immediacy of motion pictures and the striking image sequences often produced can inspire designers to structure layouts and publications in similar ways. For example, this book discusses the importance of pace and narrative in a piece of work, aspects that can be structured like a movie. Pace and intensity could be changed and manipulated through the use of different treatments for layouts, images and text.

Culture

The majority of designs are produced to serve a present need so the existing culture becomes a common reference or influence for a piece of work aiming to appeal to its target audience. Designers use the elements of popular culture such as colours, typefaces and accepted social norms or taboos in their work to reflect the times they live in and to appeal to the communal mind of the population. At the cutting edge, this may include the use of street culture's vernacular to create designs with elements from the constantly moving pulse of society.

Designs are produced based on a variety of influences including art, music, magazines, collections of objects or paintings such as *Composition* by Russian modernist abstract painter Wassily Kandinsky (left). Magazines, in particular, tend to appropriate from a wide range of influences to produce visually dynamic covers and spreads (right). Designers also glean inspiration from random objects and items such as these Russian dolls (below).

Magazines

There are many publications for and about the design industry. These are not only useful for viewing works of other designers, but for keeping abreast with movements, trends and technologies within the industry in general.

Industry publications also allow a designer to build a contact book and keep track of who is working where, which may be useful in the future. These publications often also provide relevant information on the administrative side of the design business, such as legal issues, tax advice and copyright, in addition to details of various organisational bodies and associations.

Music

Design and music appear to have a symbiotic relationship as a designer can follow musical principles to inject pace or rhythm into a project. A designer can mimic the beats that music has through the use of large-scale images or text-free pages – interludes within the content flow, creating different beats in how page content is split between image and text pages.

Objects

Collections of objects and found items can also provide an eclectic and exciting set of influences. Designers actively seek inspiration for their work in various locations, even in their respective cities. At other times, inspiration may come from objects within their studio. These influences can creep into design decisions. Many designers like to surround themselves with interesting objects, pictures, posters and other stimuli in order to be constantly inspired.

Other areas of design

Graphic designers draw inspiration from all creative fields including other fields of design, such as furniture and interiors. Indeed, many creative people do not see themselves as being limited to one discipline. For example, the De Stijl and Bauhaus schools were involved in painting, furniture and graphic design, using common principles to guide their work across different disciplines and media.

Design as problem solving

———— An important part of the design process deals with overcoming creative, practical or economic obstacles. This may sound straightforward, but often, the problem is ephemeral – a feeling that something is not right with a design. Problem solving entails working through the various elements of a design and not simply making assumptions as to what the problem is.

Questions not answers

Often, a design problem is not what we initially think it is and it is frequently a good idea to start by questioning the very question that we are asking. It is easy to assume that design is the answer to solving a problem, but doing this may mean that the wrong question has been asked and is in turn answered.

In the case of advertising, there may be several ways to increase the sales of a product. One is to redesign its visual or advertising images, but this is not the only way. The real problem may be that the product does not meet the requirements of its <u>target audience</u> and may instead require a repositioning within the market rather than a redesign. As there is more than one solution to a problem, there is also often more than one question that needs to be asked. It may be the case that a client who engages a designer to solve a problem may not have asked themselves the right question to begin with.

Macro and micro problems

Macro problems are those that affect the big picture, such as overall product strategy. On the other hand, micro problems are smaller in scale and affect specific elements within a strategy.

Different problems require different solutions with varying skill sets required. How to produce a complex book design within a certain extent or page count is a different exercise from creating a new brand image, although both are undertaken by the design discipline. Design is one element of the macro picture and is a function that sits besides product development, advertising, marketing, public relations, production and distribution. Some clients may think that design can solve every problem, but ultimately, design cannot rectify what is essentially a non-design problem.

Target audience
The main recipient or demographic of a message or a product.

University of East Anglia

University of East Anglia (above)

The logo for the University of East Anglia was created by Blast and features a three-letter ligature of the UEA initials. Note how the crossbars of the E and A unite to form what could be crosshairs, implying focus and precision, while at the same time resembling a shining star or beacon implying brilliance.

Dyson (above)

Thirteen's design for a staff communication booklet for Dyson features a simple split of its name that produces a forward-looking and humourous result.

Handrail (right)

Jog Design's colour sample pack for Handrail ingeniously uses an architectural material – standard twinwall polycarbonate – as a device for carrying colour samples instead of the square samples previously sent out. Putting the colour sample on a tube gives a truer colour representation to clients and architects due to the way light falls on its curved surface, making colours appear darker in the shadow area and lighter where full light is received.

Methods of problem-solving

There are different approaches that can be taken when thinking about design. A design problem can be approached from various perspectives using different methodologies, which can all aid a designer to develop a workable solution. The approach taken will depend upon the nature of the job in hand, as well as the experience and preferences of the designer. Experienced creative designers refrain from following the same processes every time; using different methods allows a problem to be viewed from different perspectives, which provides a means for the unexpected to enter into the piece.

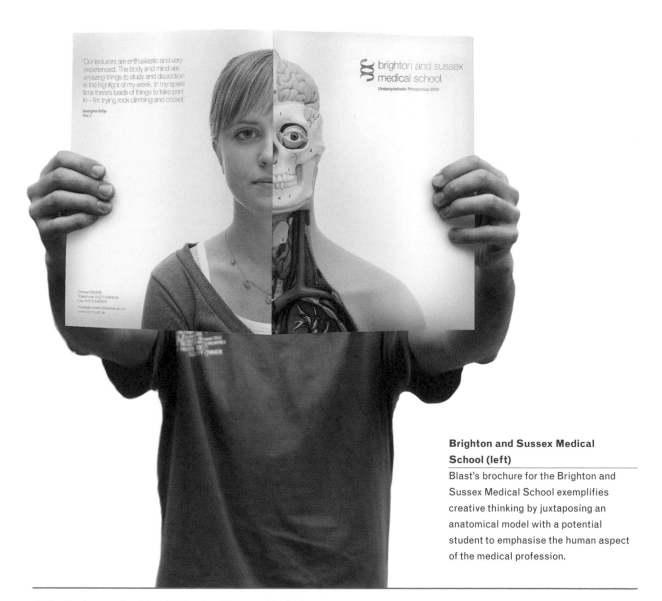

Brighton and Sussex Medical School (left)

Blast's brochure for the Brighton and Sussex Medical School exemplifies creative thinking by juxtaposing an anatomical model with a potential student to emphasise the human aspect of the medical profession.

Empirical

A designer can break down a problem into its constituent parts to view its elements scientifically and see how they function in relation to one another. This approach reveals the important relationships between different elements and the functionality required between them.

Chunking

A complex problem can be simplified by breaking it down into smaller chunks and working on it a chunk at a time. Finding solutions to each small chunk may provide a better perspective from which to decide how to piece the elements back together in a coherent way, and eventually solve the overall design problem.

Clustering

While many clients ask designers to make a job stand out from their competitors, the concept of clustering counters this and states that a design should fit into the established visual pattern of a particular product niche or industry.

For example, on a street that houses various estate agents – a cluster – that have conservative visual identities, developing an entirely different brand could be a risky strategy as people tend to respond to what they are familiar with. Market research often supports this idea showing that consumers prefer new products that conform to their perceptions of their old favourites. However, there are opportunities for designs that break with the established trend after careful analysis and testing.

Lateral thinking

Lateral thinking is a term devised by psychologist Edward de Bono. It involves changing the concepts and perceptions one uses to approach a problem in order to find a solution. Lateral thinking is used to stimulate people and to escape the established paradigms they dearly hold on to, which may prevent them from finding workable solutions to the problems they face. This method entails moving from the predictable to something unexpected.

Opposition

Thinking about the absolute opposite of the standard or accepted idea is a way of changing perspective and inverting paradigms, and can produce workable results. For example, if food packaging for a particular product category is typically red, why not try green?

Top down and bottom up

These are analytical approaches appropriated from information technology development, with the former looking at a problem from the system perspective and then drilling down to add detail in specific areas. The bottom up approach focuses on the basic elements first and works upwards to link everything together as part of a system.

Substitution

Substitution refers to the replacement of one element of the design and/or design process with an element from another creative or production process in order to benefit from the different way that tasks are structured or performed.
For example, the mass production techniques established by Henry Ford in the early twentieth century have been applied to most industries, leading to developments such as fast food. In design, drafting tables were substituted by personal computers that provided greater flexibility, allowing designers to produce designs quickly while engaging in more trial and error. Designers sometimes substitute their computer technology for former ways of freehand drafting, Letrasets and paste-up boards in order to produce innovative designs.

Creative thinking

—————— Graphic design is a creative process that does more than simply respond to a client's brief. There are many ways to respond to a brief and the demands it contains, and each will provide solutions that produce differing levels of success. Creative design explores the wider themes in order to find the optimum solution to a brief.

Creative approaches

The first step in the creative process is to use broad-based thinking to challenge accepted paradigms and assumptions. This process may involve deconstruction to dismantle accepted ways of doing things, which could inhibit finding a solution. Designers can use various tools to obtain different perspectives and identify the most important elements to communicate. Such methods may help a designer arrive at a novel solution, whether the ultimate aim is to produce a magazine spread or a chair.

User-centred design (UCD)

The needs, desires and limitations of the user are placed at the centre of every stage of the design process and require designers to foresee how users are likely to use the resulting product. This method focuses on the goals and tasks associated with the use of a design, rather than focusing on the needs, desires and limitations of the user.

KISS (Keep it simple, stupid)

This principle highlights the fact that simplicity is a desirable objective in producing effective designs.

Python philosophy

This philosophy was derived from ideas presented by Tim Peters in 'The Zen of Python', such as 'beautiful is better than ugly', 'explicit is better than implicit', 'simple is better than complex', 'complex is better than complicated', 'sparse is better than dense', 'readability counts', 'special cases are not special enough to break the rules', 'practicality beats purity', 'errors should never pass silently' and 'refuse the temptation to guess'.

TIMTOWTDI

This means that 'there is more than one way to do it' and follows the belief that a problem may have several different, but equally valid, solutions.

Ockham's razor

This involves methodological reductionism, which seeks to pare back elements that are not really needed to produce something simpler, and in so doing, reduces the risk of introducing inconsistencies, ambiguities and redundancies.

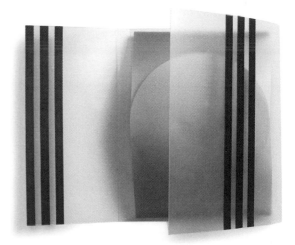

Harrison Pursey (above)

The design of this frisbee was created by Blast for recruitment agency Harrison Pursey. As part of a brand development, it uses the witty motto 'seek find fetch' to underline the direct nature of its approach to placing go-getters. The frisbee also represents something fun and memorable.

Kevin Leighton (below)

The stationery designed by Mark Studio, Manchester, for photographer Kevin Leighton aims to capture the client's distinctive personality in a staightforward and unexpected way.

Adidas press folder (above)

Jog Design's press folder for sportswear manufacturer Adidas incorporates the brand into its physical aspect. The three stripes on the front are not only decorative – they are magnetic strips that hold the folder shut.

Wit and humour

—— Graphic design has enormous scope to present and exploit wit graphically as it seeks to communicate ideas to viewers. Humour is often very memorable and aids retention of the message. However, it is not something that always goes hand in hand with graphic design. As a discipline, design can take itself too seriously and can come across as self-referential, formal and overbearing.

Wit in graphic design

Wit is a sub-category of humour, something that is intended to spark a merry reaction, lighten our state of mind and ease our emotions. Humour is often presented in graphic design as the visual portrayal or equivalent of language, a phrase or expression. As in real life, there are people who handle wit in design with ease and panache, and those who misfire or use it inappropriately. Jack Somerford's Southwestern Typographics t-shirt design uses wit by setting the word Helvetica in the Garamond font. It is a visual joke that not everyone will understand as it is aimed at designers who will appreciate the irony it presents. Wit and humour are relative – in order to understand the joke, you have to understand the elements and circumstances that form it.

Wit is often considered as a graphic way of expressing ideas. Wit and ideas can and do overlap when the subjective conditions are right as an idea may not be witty in and of itself, but only when the context in which it is presented makes it so. The idea of making a tall promotional brochure is not witty, but when the client is a clothing company for tall people it could be witty to use such a format.

Wit is usually expressed through the aid of other graphic devices, such as those listed on the opposite page.

Garamond Helvetica

Restaurant Design

The cover for Bethan Ryder's book, *Restaurant Design*, was designed by Blast. It incorporates a witty trompe l'oeil that uses an image of a plate on the front and back. The publisher's logo appears at the foot of the spine but also where we would expect to see the brand mark of the plate manufacturer – amusing yet understated.

Juxtaposition

Juxtaposition puts together related or dissimilar objects in such a way that a relationship is established between them. This may be due to the fact that they have certain qualities in common, or are very different and have clashing qualities.

Transformation

A designer can show transformation by presenting a perception of altered time, placement, scale or other action. For example, juxtaposing images such as a caterpillar and a butterfly can present commonly understood metaphors and transformations in a humorous way.

Pun

This is a phrase that intentionally exploits the similarity between words that sound similar, or different meanings of the same word, as a type of word play.

Trompe l'oeil

Literally meaning 'trick of the eye', this is an image technique that fools the eye into seeing something that is not really there.

Two-in-one

This occurs when two messages are given in a single communication, such as by combining two items that would not normally belong together. This double meaning, or double entendre, is often used to add humour to a design.

Homage

Homage may be used wittily by copying the essence of something well-established and recognised in popular culture and then giving it a humorous twist. This could be a classic work of art, a corporate logo or a well-publicised incident involving famous people.

Rebus

This is a visual puzzle in which the participant has to decode a message that is presented as a series of pictures representing different words, numbers and/or syllables.

uinness

This Guinness poster by Abram Games combines the initial G of the brand name with the product use, in this case, having a drink. In this example, the G is a gift as its characteristics are also used to form a face and a pint of beer.

Wigan Little Theatre (below)
This identity was created by Mark Studio, Manchester for Wigan Little Theatre and uses a small format to create a distinctive and charming brand identity for the amateur theatre company that self-mockingly refers to its diminutive size and name.

Manchester Comedy Festival (above)

Pictured are posters created by Studio Mark for the Manchester Comedy Festival that feature portrait photographs of people looking unhappy, the opposite of what you would expect for such an event. Here, the creative thinking veils the seemingly incongruous images with humour, in that the people are funny because they look so miserable.

Same but different (below)

Webb & Webb's brochure for Coventry University features still images taken from video and then printed on transparent stock. The stills have die-cut edges that create both a facsimile of film and match the material cut away for the wiro binding.

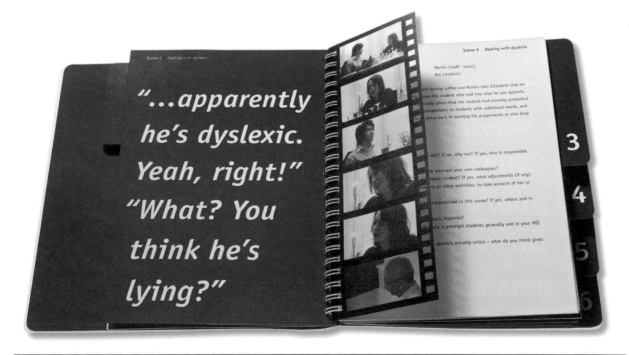

Layers of meaning

———— Design can carry several layers of meanings or different ideas by using various graphic devices. These layers can convey an idea beyond the simple formal presentation of information in a piece of communication as they are able to connect with broader ideas and references held by the target readers.

Intervention

A graphic designer can add to the power of a message through graphic intervention that emphasises the idea being communicated. The example below provides a simplistic example of this.

It starts with a word – poverty – and then adds to it to develop the idea represented in a way that goes beyond the mere choice of font. To emphasise the idea, the graphic treatments can be altered and new treatments incorporated to reinforce the meaning of the word.

poverty

Type
A simple word has a literal meaning.

poverty

Emphasis
Using a heavier font gives extra power to the meaning.

pove⊥ty

Intentional miⱭspelling
By reversing one of the letters, a lack of education is implied, which may be due to poverty.

poverty

Typographic stories
The use of a mono-spaced, typewriter-style font creates the impression of a lack of resources.

p●verty

Substitution
Here, the 'o' has been replaced with the image of a coin to reinforce the fact that poverty is related to money (or the lack of it).

Infantilism
This child-like font is a powerful communication implying that poverty hits children worst.

Mirage (above and right)

This identity for Mirage was created by Jog Design and it features the distinctive capital of the logotype on the cover. The logotype was created by burning away the edges of the typeface to imitate how the edges of an object are burnt away when you look at them against the sun, thus playing on word 'mirage'. The type also reads the wrong way, as though it has burnt through from the preceding page.

National Assessment Agency (NAA) (right)

This folder and inserts, including posters, were created by The Team for a campaign to recruit examiners, markers and moderators of GCSE and 'A' levels for the NAA. Feedback from examiners formed the core messages for the campaign – 'Examine their future' and 'Behind every paper there's a student'. Research showed the messages rang true and helped attract more than double the targeted number of applicants.

Development and experimentation

———— Design is a creative process that encapsulates experimentation and the development of visual and physical ideas. The starting point for development and experimentation is the job's brief. Once this has been agreed, the design team can start working up ideas to fulfil it.

Experimentation in design

Personal computers and digital technology have driven the development of graphic design over the last 20 years, and have given designers great flexibility to experiment creatively by making it easy to change a design on-screen, incorporate different effects, draw new type forms and so forth. However, experimentation and the design development process do not have to be technology-driven; many designers benefit from a craft-based approach, returning to pre-computer practices to produce new ideas.

A craft-based approach sees designers getting hands-on with various materials that provide the chance to focus on tactile qualities, folding, cut-outs and other aspects that are difficult to visualise by looking at a computer screen. The last chapter in this book refers to a basic kit that can be used to experiment in this way.

Uncomfortable truths (right)

This is a V&A Museum poster for a slave trade exhibition.
NB: Studio's design features an ink-drawn image representing the travel aspect of the trade as people were forcibly relocated.

Adidas (above, right and below)

Jog Design's brochure for Adidas appropriated and re-purposed the idea of a map so that the document could be browsed in different directions without the need to open it out. The format allows the reader to peel back the shoe to see it operating at various levels and in different conditions. The folding mechanism also creates three strong lines that reflect the stripes of the Adidas brand.

The sketches below were made for the website shown opposite. These were used to establish basic spatial relationships and to determine the feel and look of the pages prior to programming.

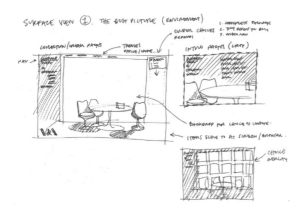

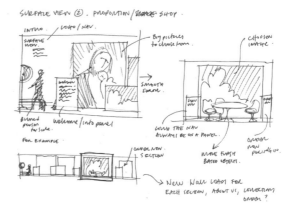

Sketching

Sketching refers both to drawing images with a pencil and the process of thinking ideas through to build and refine them. Although technology has equipped designers with many electronic aids, sketching remains a valuable design tool to develop and rough-out ideas for answering a brief.

Sketching as drawing

Sketching as the art of drawing is an essential design tool allowing a designer to quickly outline the visual elements of a design and capture an idea in the moment that it materialises. Sketching means a designer can quickly articulate an idea to a client without having to produce a complete design. A visual record of that idea can then be worked up in full detail at the studio.

Sketching as thinking

Sketching out the thumbnails of the pages of a publication provides a visual aid that helps a designer to plan the project, its pace and the placement of text and images. This makes it easier to conceptualise the final publication in a way that can be easily altered before starting the detailed design.

Once the detailed design has begun, it is easy to become bogged down in the details and overlook aspects, such as the flow of a publication and the narrative that unfolds on successive pages.

Sketching is immediate, full of energy and it can capture the quintessential elements of the design. It is also cheap – ideas can be drawn, dismissed, reworked, refined or thrown away very quickly and at little cost before the designer even sits down at the computer, which can save time in the long run.

Thumbnails

Thumbnails are small-scale representations of the pages of a publication and can be used to start and form the basis of the final work by setting the pace of a project, and the location of specific elements. A book, for instance, is not just a series of pages – the pages have a sequence, flow and relationships with each other, which can only be seen in this reduced size.

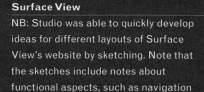
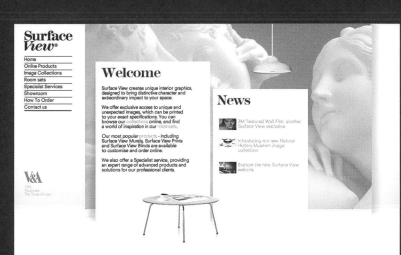

Surface View

NB: Studio was able to quickly develop ideas for different layouts of Surface View's website by sketching. Note that the sketches include notes about functional aspects, such as navigation and backdrops.

Art direction

——— Art direction is a process that guides the creation of the visual elements of a design. An art director harnesses and integrates the various elements within a design to produce a certain look and feel for the resulting artwork so that it contains the required expressions and conveys the appropriate messages.

The art director

An art director orchestrates the visual creative processes of a project and decides the aesthetic that a design will have. An art director does not take the photographs, produce the illustrations, build the sets or style the models in a photo shoot, but he or she will determine the overall direction and visual goal of the project. The direction provided by the art director will be the focus of the creative effort of the team working on the job, which may include a photographer, an illustrator and a developer of computer imagery.

Graphic designers occupy a central role within the design process, coordinating and bringing together the various design elements that are commissioned from individuals with different specialisations. This central position means that it is common for them to also occupy the role of art director. A designer will have a mental map of what they want the final job to look like and will communicate this idea to photographers, illustrators, stylists etc, in order to achieve the required look. This may involve broadly determining the colour palette to be used in addition to being on-hand to resolve ad hoc queries during the production of the different elements.

Art direction is focused on achieving a specific visual result, which may be inspired by influences as diverse as current trends and fashions, a historical or futuristic perspective, a particular theme, such as advanced technology or a pastoral scene, or an attitude or emotion, depending upon the results required. It is the art director's job to ensure that this happens.

Successful art direction results in a coherent and unified design that the target audience will find credible and/or attractive. The designs that result from this process can be very powerful, and it is art direction that is responsible for producing the images that add so much value to brand development.

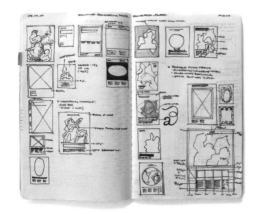

Brindabella

These are images from a project created by 3 Deep Design
for the visual positioning of *Brindabella*, a performance piece by
BalletLab, which shows the project-development cycle from the
initial sketches of the visual concept (top left) to the set
construction for the photoshoot (top right), the creation of the
hero image (above) and the final poster (right) that resulted
from this process. This example shows the amount of work that
can be involved in creating a visual identity and the importance
of art direction to harness the different elements and disciplines
involved to achieve that end. Graphic designers are increasingly
at the centre of the art direction process to ensure that the
vision sketched at the concept stage is realised as intended.

Hero image
The key image that a visual campaign pivots on – the focal or defining point.

Prototyping

——— Getting from a design idea to a realised project is not always straightforward and may require a considerable amount of prototyping to get things right. Once the design team has a consolidated idea of how to answer a brief, prototyping provides an opportunity for testing some of the proposed solutions without going to the expense of full development.

Different prototypes for different design areas

Graphic design is broad and varied, so the prototyping methods used will vary greatly from one job to another. A web programmer may get colleagues to test their work on a variety of different computers and operating software before a website goes live, while an environmental communications designer may produce different versions of signage to test its readability under specific light and weather conditions. The following are some items to consider when prototyping. Bear in mind that these are not exhaustive as every job can present specific issues.

Print – wet proofs

Print jobs require proofing as the results may vary from one stock to another. Various proofs or test prints can be performed to check everything from text to layout and colour reproduction. A final test print, called a match print or Chromalin, is typically used to see the final design at the right resolution and colour. This is the proof that a printer adheres to, although it is not printed on the actual printing stock.

The only way to really see how something will print is to obtain a wet proof that is printed on the same press that will be used to print the job, using the same plates and the same stock. However, other factors affect the final result, such as the environment, lighting conditions, printing plate pressure, ink film thickness, humidity and drying conditions. While a wet proof provides the closest match possible, the minder who monitors the press has to match something that is dry (the wet proof) to something that is wet (the printed piece leaving the running press), which means that colour variation can still occur.

It is also advisable to obtain a printer's dummy for a job (see page 79). This is a format mock-up of the final printed piece that is used to check the binding, how the pages fold, creep and other aspects that affect the physical form of a publication.

The weight of this product is being checked for postage considerations and to see if it feels substantial enough.

Here, the feel of the paper (textural quality), is being checked, as well as whether it tears easily.

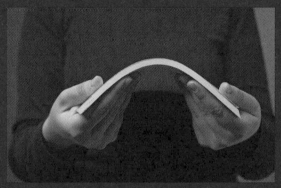

Bending the stock allows one to check its flex and to what extent it resumes its original shape.

Different stocks will produce different spine widths due to their caliper – making a dummy text block essential.

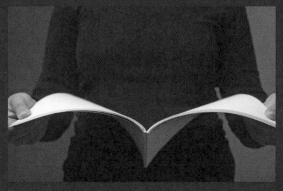

The binding method is checked using the stock to see if it opens flat enough to use and read.

Any special elements or treatments, such as gatefolds or throw-outs, should be checked to see if they work properly.

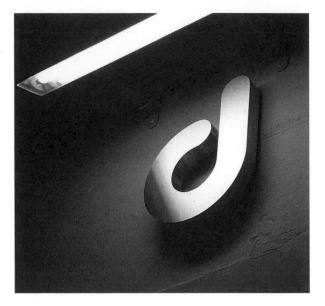

Chandos (right)

Thirteen designed this signage for dental practice, Chandos. The 'C' letterform from the client's name is modern and discreet, and is set in a sans serif font with equal stroke weight. Notice how the letter has been extruded into an ascender that turns the letter into a 'd' that indicates 'dentist'. The production of signage such as this requires prototyping as what works on paper may be less effective and disappear visually within the built environment where it is to be used. Prototyping gives a designer the opportunity to see how the physical manifestation of the design works in situ.

Packaging – mock-ups

Most packaged items are three-dimensional and do not exist as flat designs. The easiest and most effective means of prototyping a packaged item is to make a three-dimensional mock-up that allows a designer to see how the design looks as an object; how the different sides relate to each other; and the physical attributes it has, such as strength.

A mock-up allows a designer to put the item in context and modify the design in order to optimise it. For example, an item that looks striking and bold on paper can fade into the background when placed in the context of a shelf in a busy supermarket. The mock-up also allows a designer to test how readable the text is at different distances and under different lighting conditions. These dummies can also be used for market research to gauge how target consumers will respond to, and interact with, the packaging. A designer will look at the front, back, and sides of the flat form of the packaging, while a user will see several sides simultaneously as they hold the package in their hands.

Exhibitions – maquettes and models

Maquettes and models use large-scale prototypes that need carefully determined proportions so that viewers can read and understand any directions clearly. Here, the pragmatic aspects of prototyping come to the fore and a designer needs to constantly review the fundamentals and ask if the user can use the design as intended. For example, when using signage such as directional instructions, a designer must ask if it is clear which way a person is supposed to go. Is the information clearly printed? Is the purpose of shapes and arrows unmistakable?

An exhibition space involves broader considerations and a designer needs to consider the collective narrative of what is being presented – an exhibition is more than a collection of boards, objects and displays. The planning and ordering of the items creates a narrative that serves as a story or thread for a visitor to follow. These must be tested to ensure that they make sense – they must be accessible and flow smoothly. This is often done by making a maquette or model of the space to plan space usage and item placement.

Radar (right)

Pictured is a poster created by Mark Design, London that folds down into an A5 booklet, which presents the challenge of being engaging when viewed from a distance, yet intimate when viewed close-up. The only way to successfully achieve this combination is to use a trial-and-error approach using full-size and full-colour test pieces.

Web design – beta versions

A web design prototype is typically very close to the actual design as it is produced from the programmed pages. As websites typically include clickable links, animations, roll-over elements, sound and video, it would be difficult to test one in any other way. Reviewing a series of screen prints may be the first stage, but ultimately, these are of limited use without the ability to test the interactive elements of the actual website.

A beta version of a site is usually built to test its aesthetic and functional aspects, such as navigational anomalies where a viewer can find themselves lost or at a dead end. Once testing has been completed and all amendments made, the beta version of a website can go live and be posted on the actual pages where the public or target users can view it.

Typography – print-outs

Typography is most often checked via print-outs to ensure that the words, grammar and numerical information are correct, and that the text has the right tone and intellectual level for the target audience. This focus on getting the message and text right means that it is easy to overlook the context that the typography will be used in. For instance, while reviewing the text of a poster, it is easy to forget that it needs to be viewed from the other side of the street and not at a desk. People tend to hold proofs closer to their face than they would a book, so what may be a readable typesize on a proof may not be so readable when reading a book, due to the typesize or font clarity.

Commissioning art

——— Artwork embraces various visual elements that are not always created by the designer, such as illustration and photography. Design is a collaborative process involving many relationships, and commissioning presents rich and varied opportunities for designers to realise their creativity by harnessing external skills as needed.

Why commission?

While the array of modern technology and services, such as photo libraries, means that designers have access to, or can produce, a vast range of images, there are still many occasions when artwork will need to be commissioned. While some designers also write, illustrate and take photographs, it is unlikely that they will be able to produce every element that a design requires. There are many jobs that require additional specialist input. Illustrators, photographers, sign writers, typographers and copywriters specialise in the production of specific outputs in diverse ways. The commissioning of artwork allows a designer to access the broad range of creative styles and techniques that the practitioners have, which can add different creative elements into the design mix, therefore allowing a job to have a more sophisticated and robust resolve.

The commissioning process

Commissioning artwork is not necessarily an easy or quick process, but neither is it difficult, complicated or slow. Commissioning should not be viewed as a chance to offload work, but as a creative challenge in itself. The process can be broken down into four stages: selection, commissioning, development and completion.

Selection

The selection process involves researching who is available to produce the required artwork, including their styles and rates. While it is convenient to use tried and tested contacts, it is important to be aware of other professionals who are available and the type of work they specialise in, just in case regular contacts are unavailable or a job requires something completely different. This first stage often involves viewing websites, contacting photographic agents and other contacts to help direct the search so that a shortlist can be made. This is particularly true when commissioning photography, illustration or screen-printing.

Somerset House, London (left)

This fold-out poster created for Somerset House in London features illustrations by C'est Moi Ce Soir, which offer a light-hearted guide to ice skating in the courtyard of the building. Different illustration styles are available to graphic designers and it is important to select one that is compatible with the project and the message to be conveyed. Research Studios interpreted the brief by showing ice skating as a fun, sporting pastime enjoyed by many children, and this is reflected in the colourful, rudimentary illustrations.

Commissioning

Commissioning involves agreeing the job parameters for the artwork, such as the brief, cost, delivery time, the process to be used and what the deliverables will be. For example, when commissioning illustrations, it must be agreed whether items will be produced in pencil, watercolour or India ink. It is important to formalise the commission at this stage, and the process will depend on the relationship you have with the provider.

It is always advisable to note the relevant details agreed on paper, particularly if artwork is commissioned from a new source, so that there is a document to refer to in case of disputes later on. Where there is an established working relationship, a commission may be as informal as an email requesting a job to the same specifications as a previous one. Some commissions may be agreed with a handshake while others are established by a formal, signed contract.

Development and completion

The development stage is marked by the beginning of artwork production, such as preparatory sketches or prototypes. Depending on the complexity and budget of the job, it is not unusual to move from the commissioning stage to completion through intermediary stages that give both parties a chance to make further decisions on the artwork before the time and expense is taken to produce it.

Completion marks the end of the process where the commissioned artwork is delivered to the client. If this matches the expectations as specified in the commissioning agreement – whether verbal or written – the process ends and the producer invoices the client. Work that is unsuitable or off-specification may be so for a number of reasons: there may have been insufficient dialogue during the development stage; the brief established during the commissioning stage was insufficient or inaccurate; or perhaps an inappropriate candidate was picked at the selection stage. As designers are usually in charge of the commissioning process, they are normally responsible for any shortcomings with the final artwork.

Commissioning illustration

Illustration encompasses a broad spectrum of techniques and styles as different illustrators work with different processes and use different media. They can be figurative, abstract, collage-based, computer-generated, etc. It may be necessary to obtain portfolios from several different practitioners in order to get a sense of their style and find one that is suitable for the job in hand.

Drugs – Facing Facts (left and below)

Webb & Webb's design for the Royal Society for the Encouragement of the Arts, Manufacturers & Commerce (RSA) features duotone illustrations by Chris Brown that have a primitive, understated, lino-cut feel that provides a plain and balanced counterpoint to the importance and severity of the subject matter. Although beautifully typeset, the publication would be dull without the intervention of the graphic illustrations that clearly enliven and define its different areas.

Commissioning photography

Photography is a broad and diverse discipline where practitioners tend to specialise in specific areas or fields such as fashion, advertising, sports and reportage. As photographing a car requires a different skill set to a fashion shoot, a designer will need to select someone who is familiar with the requirements of the brief's subject matter. Many photographers are represented by agents who can provide a copy of their portfolio, and it is increasingly common for photographers to have websites to showcase their style, subject matter and technical expertise.

Made in Medway (above and left)

Steve Rowland's *Made in Medway* title features portraits of local artists taken by photographer Rikard Österlund. Subjects are shot facing the camera, making the reader feel included in the scene. The book was sponsored by Medway Renaissance with support from UCCA Rochester.

Commissioning moving image

Moving images often need to be outsourced as not all agencies have in-house capabilities to provide or generate these. In spite of technological advances, it is not always practical or cost-effective to have specialists in-house. However, specialist firms can be commissioned to provide these services. By providing services to many clients, these firms spread the cost of the equipment and technology they require in addition to generating real expertise by working exclusively in moving-image production.

The image above shows how different parts of the scene are masked off to create a sense of movement in the 3D film.

WoWvx (below)
The following stills from a two-minute film produced by INTRO for Philips is used to showcase its WoWvx 3D display that allowed viewers to enjoy 3D without the need for special glasses. Featuring dancing showgirls, boxing and blockbuster action sequences, the colourful, action-packed film was created using different film/3D techniques to show viewers the excitement and power that 3D brings to the TV screen. The display is comprised of a sheet of transparent lenses fixed on an LCD screen. Each lens carries a slightly different offset of the same image. In the same way your two eyes receive a slightly different angle of the same image, this offset is the 'measurement' system that our brains use as a way of judging depth and how we sense the three dimensionality of space.

Commissioning typography

Typography may be commissioned for typographical jobs that go beyond typesetting. This is particularly the case when the creation of a single mark, or even an entire alphabet, is of paramount importance to the development of a unique message, such as a revamp of a brand. Commissioning typography allows a brand or message to be presented with a unique character set that differentiates it from any other communication. When a new typeface is being commissioned for a job, the team working on it usually collects examples from existing typefaces or designs to focus on type characteristics and personalities, which serve as a reference for the one to be created.

Dow Jones (above and right)

Pictured is a brand guideline manual created by Marque for a commission from the Dow Jones news agency. Dalton Maag, a specialist type foundry, was commissioned to develop a font for this project. The font helps define the identity and personality of the news service, giving a unique visual voice that adds strength to the company and the information it publishes.

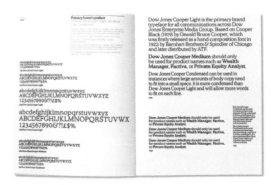

Chapter 4
Delivering the message

_____ Graphic design is presented to its target audience through a wide range of media from printed flyers to posters and websites. As such, this chapter addresses how varying messages are conveyed using a vast array of techniques, tools and methods. It looks at the end results of the design process and the work that the audience, often the general public, interacts with.

This chapter focuses on the various platforms that designers have at their disposal to deliver strong and specific messages – from print and screen through to environmental design where a piece actually forms part of the physical environment.

Jonathan Crisp (opposite)

Ziggurat's design for food products company Jonathan Crisp uses a personality-led approach to create visual disruption, grab attention and create a 'smile in the mind' of the consumer. The use of caricatures by Paul Baker and the signature font injects personality and humour that tap into latent associations of discernment and snobbery in a tongue-in-cheek way.

<u>**Areas looked at in this chapter**</u>

Print [p110] / Direct mail [p116] / Information design [p118] / Packaging [p120] / Screen design [p122] / Environmental design [p126]

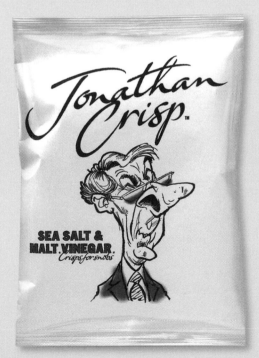

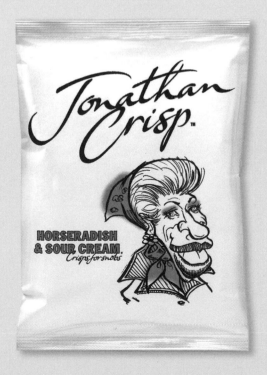

Print

——— Printing is a collective term that refers to the various methods used to apply ink to a substrate such as offset lithography, screen-printing, gravure, letterpress, hot-metal, lino cut, thermography, ink-jet and laser printing. These methods enable text and images to be printed on to a wide range of substrates from paper and board, to ceramics and textiles.

The printing process

Printing is a process that is widely used to produce books, magazines and other publications. The variety of different printing processes available gives a designer a wide range of flexibility in the finish, which can be obtained in the final product and the print run possible.

In addition to putting ink on stock, the different processes can also give a job other characteristics that result from the process itself. For example, the pressure used by the letterpress process leaves subtle indentations in the stock and causes subtle differences inthe amount of ink deposited on to the stock. Thermography and screen-printing produce characters that have a slightly raised surface. All these processes add tactile elements to a design.

The printing process is often overlooked when a job is being designed for print, but a designer must take into account the printing process to ensure that visual impact is optimised.

The way the different inks print in the standard four-colour printing process can be altered to produce different visual effects, as can techniques such as overprinting, surprinting and the addition of shiners.

The print process selected for a job and how it is specified has a big impact on the cost of the job and the schedule for its production. Creative use of the print process means that a designer can overcome some of the restrictions of budgetary constraints, which may limit a job to having two colours rather than four.

The choice of printing method is determined by several factors, although for the majority of jobs the most important are printing cost and print run quantity. Each printing method has particular limiting characteristics that differ from process to process. These may affect printing speed, the number of colours printed, the types of paper stock and the paper format or size.

**Editions de la Martinière
(above and left)**

This is *La Terra, Vue du Ciel* by Yann Arthus-Bertrand, designed by Research Studios. It contains pictures of the earth taken from the air. This collector's edition has an exceptionally large format with the long side measuring 70cm, providing ample space to let the images come to life and impress the reader.

Acordis (above)

The Vast Agency's brochure for Acordis features subtle increments of ink to create a soft, delicate print with which to present information about fine fabrics. The care and attention taken over the printing reflects the care and attention taken over the fabrics.

Internal communications

In addition to communicating to the world at large, many companies and organisations also generate a wide range of internal communications for their employees, both in print and web format. Here, the target audience already has an understanding of the product and the culture of the organisation issuing the communication. As a result, content is presented towards the employees' perspective so that they feel included in the ongoing debate about the direction and progress of the entity. Such publications can often include more technical information.

Dyson internal communications (left and below)

Pictured are spreads from the staff magazine created by Thirteen for home products producer, Dyson. Each issue of the magazine is visually different and presents innovative, engaging and inspirational messages to reinforce the culture of the company and the nature of its approach to product design. As this is an internal publication, it addresses an audience that already understands the company's products and messages. However, it still needs to be engaging for its messages to be effectively communicated.

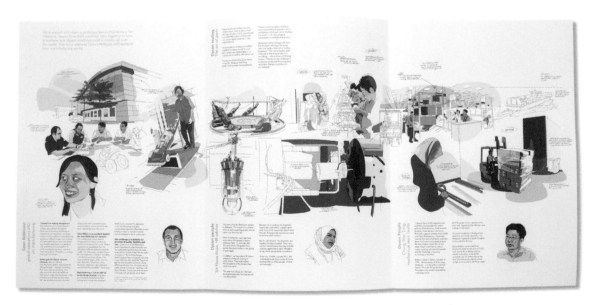

National Maritime Museum (right)

These simple icon-based covers by Mark Design, London result in an engaging identity for the publishing department of the National Maritime Museum. Instead of using traditional images of the sea, icons that individually refer to the sea were used, collectively creating the sensation of a wave breaking over a beach.

Axeman Lullaby (right)

Pictured are posters created by 3 Deep Design for performance company BalletLab that feature arresting monotone images, which capture the essence of the Axeman Lullaby show. The image styling suggests blood spatter that combines with the fearful look of the character in the image to inform the public about the nature of the show. The use of black rather than red ink prevents the image from appearing too grisly.

City of Light, Krems
(right and below)

The City of Light brochure designed by Büro X for the city of Krems uses yellow as a <u>flood</u> <u>colour</u> that bleeds off the page edges. The colour also merges into some of the photography.

Flood colour
Full-bleed colour that flows off some or all sides of the printed piece.

Annual reports

Annual reports provide an important source of work for graphic designers. They are more than just about figures – they provide a valuable means of communication and are used to inform readers, shareholders and staff of the organisation's direction and aspirations. Annual reports are often designed with a particular theme, or tell a story about the company's objectives.

Channel 4 (left and below)
NB: Studio designed this report for Channel 4. It includes <u>eclectic</u> spreads that inform people about what the station does. The financial information is presented more soberly at the end of the publication and it is printed on a different paper stock. The report was also accompanied by a series of posters.

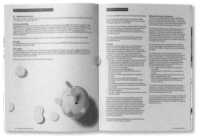
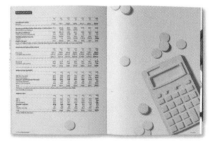

Eclectic
The use of material, images or content from a range of different sources or styles.

Direct mail

—— Direct mail is a form of marketing that attempts to present potential consumers with a message regarding a specific product or service rather than simply raising the profile of a brand, which is the aim of advertising. Direct mail can be in print or electronic form and both are sent 'direct' to an end user to elicit a buying response for a specific product or service.

Direct communication

Marketing and advertising messages for a brand generally raise its profile, whereas direct mail aims to steer consumers to a specific buying action. For example, Apple's advertising supports its overall approach to product creation, while its direct mail informs consumers of new products and accessories that they can buy.

Direct mail has two common forms: HTML emails that can click through to websites or <u>micro sites</u>, and printed communications called 'door drop' mailouts. Both are usually targeted using demographic consumer information compiled from feedback forms, product registration forms, competitions, customer service forms and other similar methods that have been collated and sold to marketing firms.

Sending specific information to a pre-selected target audience increases the chance of a communicated offer being accepted. However, sending an offer to an inappropriate segment of the population will elicit little response, and could even provoke anger that sours the recipient against the company.

The increase in the quantity of direct mail sent and how firms compile consumer details has led to a growing body of law to govern the industry. In the UK, for example, a person must have subscribed to the company's product or service at some point to be sent an HTML email. The footer of such emails must give the recipient the option to not receive future communications.

Micro sites

Marketing-led website focusing on a specific product or service that is a subsidiary of the principal website of a brand. A micro website will often contain campaign-related information that is closely linked to the direct mail theme and offer. A micro website is often accessed via a link contained in an HTML email and it is where the selling company hopes to convert the interest of the consumer into a sale.

**Alan Thornton
(above and right)**

These A3 mailers are made from 3mm-thick heavy board and were produced by Jog Design for photographer Alan Thornton. They were designed to make an impact with large, creative advertising agencies by being a counterpoint to the postcards sent by most photographers. It was based on the premise that 'Alan Thornton is a rubbish photographer', with each shot being a stunning image of something discarded on the streets of London.

Corbis / Zefa (left)

This invite was for an event to relaunch Zefa, a high-end image library that Corbis had purchased. Jog Design created a high-quality, multimedia experience that a pre-defined set of invited guests could access with individual passwords. The invitation needed to compel guests to visit the site.

Information design

——— Design plays an important role in the effective communication of information. As we have seen, design can communicate very specific information in very specific ways, and this ability can be classified as information design. Information design encompasses design strategies that are geared to the dissemination of precise information for a particular end.

Focusing on precision

Many designs have to include general information that lacks precision, which can result in ambiguity. Information design aims to communicate specific and detailed messages, such as how to assemble flat-pack furniture; the dosage requirements for medicine; the date, time and location of an event; how to install computer software; or the balance to pay on a credit card. Design under these conditions serves to draw the attention to the key information so that it is unequivocal.

An invoice design may feature different text sizes to establish a hierarchy that clearly presents the total figure, or set the text against different colour backgrounds, which distinguish between payments due and payments received. The use of diagrams can often communicate better than words, which is why assembly instructions usually include pictures or illustrations. This is also the reason why many utility bills now include consumption graphs, allowing consumers to see how their rate of consumption changes from month to month.

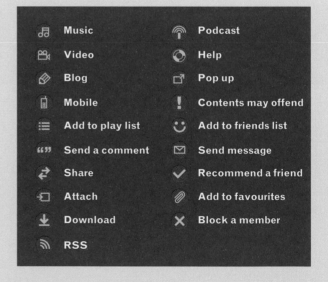

We Are Talented (above)

The icons above were designed by Research Studios as part of an identity and website design for WATT – 'We Are Talented'. The icons were produced to work at a reduced size with reduced detail for on-screen use, but they remain characterful and convey the personality of the identity.

bob (above and left)

Mobilkom Austria's corporate identity, designed by Büro X, features an unusual and reduced look based around the bob ('best of both') logo to represent best quality and best price in the competitive mobile phone market. The stylised keypad logo makes the bob brand a distinctive logotype.

Icons

Graphic elements that represent something else by reducing something to simple and instantly recognised characteristics.

Logo

A graphic symbol that is designed to represent the character of a company, product, service or other entity, such as the giant panda used by the World Wildlife Fund.

Logotype

Logotypes function by literally identifying the organisation they refer to – the logo also spells out the company name. Characters are used and styled in such a way as to give an indication of the company's strengths or culture.

Packaging

—— Packaging is a substrate that includes a printed communication, which also performs other functions such as holding and protecting its contents from damage, changes in temperature or light. Packaging design is a specialist area that spans marketing, the use of two- and three-dimensional spaces, and the placement of the item in the sales environment.

Practicalities and aesthetics

Packaging can provide different types of protection to its contents, including physical protection and insulation.

A range of different materials can be used for packaging, but cheap, lightweight materials are the most commonly used due to their practicality. They also reduce costs relating to the transportation and distribution of the product.

Packaging design for the consumer environment does not only need to consider what a product looks like individually, but also what the collective visual statement will be of several items on a shelf. The retail environment is highly competitive and retailers tend to remove lines that do not sell in high enough quantities. In a supermarket, for example, brands and their packaging have to work extremely hard to beat the competition and secure sales.

Packaging is also subject to various legal, industrial and societal conventions. For example, food packaging must contain nutritional information as it will project a brand image and target consumers that are looking for quality, security and reliability. This means some consumers may be less accepting of experimental designs as they have strong perceptions of what food products should look like.

Given the dramatic impact that packaging can have, it is an area of design in which great creativity can be seen in answer to the relatively straightforward challenge of protecting and presenting a product.

Retail environment
A place or location of trade that could function as a creative space – it can be exploited by designers to convey messages to consumers.

Daft Punk (above)

This collectible package was created for Daft Punk's Electroma DVD by Research Studios and features black printing on a metal tin. The packaging represents the dark, industrial nature of the techno-electronic music the group produces.

Superdrug (above)

Turner Duckworth's packaging redesign for Superdrug Handy Wipes use images that remind shoppers of when they might need a wipe. Each pack has a different visual prompt to illustrate that it is not only parents with small children who should have wipes to hand.

Monsters (above)

The children's haircare range for Superdrug was designed by Turner Duckworth and features monster graphics to represent the different lines. It also makes a tongue-in-cheek reference to the 'little monsters' who will use them.

Neal's Yard Remedies (above)

The Neal's Yard Remedies soap package is a box that can be reused. The box is printed with vegetable ink, which supports the ethos of the brand.

Screen design

————— Screen design is any message or communication that is ultimately delivered on, or via, a screen interface. This could be a computer screen, a Blackberry, a personal data assistant, or any similar electronic device. Screen designs have different physical considerations from printed designs.

Technological changes

As technology advances, devices tend to get smaller, more complex, more integrated with other equipment and appear in a greater variety of applications. For example, the screen interface on a telephone can now display music album covers in colour, which are far smaller than the 12-inch printed sleeves that accompanied vinyl records.

Technological change is accepted by some and resisted by others. Continuing with the musical theme, there was resistance to the use of the CD in many design quarters due to the smaller space it provides to present a design. Now, design size is increasingly influenced by pixel estate – the limited amount of pixels that a design can occupy. Each reduction in size means that the layout, type and images comprising a design have to work harder to communicate and present a clearly identifiable message. To cope with smaller sizes, fonts have been simplified so that they can be easily read, and images have to be sufficiently robust to withstand the demands of the various media they will be displayed on.

Technology also brings a greater and wider array of tools with which to tackle these problems. Screens can display an increasing gamut of colours at increasing resolutions; this simplifies a designer's task and extends the range of creative possibilities. Even relatively basic display panels prove effective, such as information panels in airports, train stations and bus terminals. It is increasingly common for such displays to be in full colour and not just an array of white light bulbs or yellow characters as in the past. However, although a screen may be able to display various colours at different resolutions, it is important to create designs that provide clear messages for the intended purpose, which may mean working well within the technological limits of a particular screen or system.

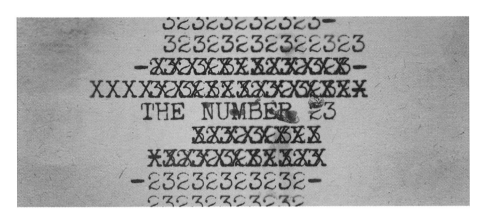

The Number 23

The opening titles for the film *The Number 23* (2007), designed by Imaginary Forces, makes use of erratic typewriter movements, seeping blood and ink blotches to suggest a haunting and dark narrative.

Television graphics

Television is something of an oddity in the graphic design world. While it is a visual medium, there are few multidisciplinary design agencies that produce work for television alongside the more traditional forms of design. There are exceptions, however.

Graphic design contributes to clearly defined areas or activities within television production that tend to have a high graphic content, such as the opening and closing credits of a show. Traditionally, the content of a TV programme was sandwiched between the credits without any graphic intervention, with programmes interspersed by commercials and station idents, such as those used by the BBC in the UK since the 1950s.

Idents, or channel identifications, are the short five- to ten-second sequences that show the viewer which channel they are watching. These may be combined with brand reinforcement and promotion.

Graphic content in TV began to increase with the increasing popularity of MTV in the 1980s, which was characterised by the repeated use of innovative and creative station idents, and other on-screen graphic elements and moving pictures.

Technological development has facilitated the use of graphics in TV and film productions, leading to the development of agencies that specialise in its creation. An example of this is Imaginary Forces, an entertainment and design company based in Hollywood and New York. Imaginary Forces is a leading exponent of graphics for films and has a list of film credits, including the Jim Carrey film *The Number 23* (2007).

Idents

A brief film or image sequence that identifies the channel or station that a television viewer is watching. Typically run between programmes, idents have become increasingly creative and form part of channel identity branding.

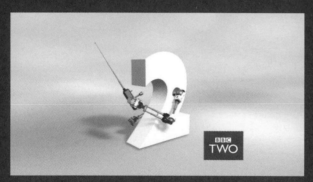

BBC idents (left)

These three stills are from idents created by Lambie-Nairn for the BBC.

The BBC One idents (top) use the globe, a constant feature of the ident since the 1950s, as a key visual feature. Based on the insight that BBC One 'brings the whole world to every corner of the nation,' the globe was given a new lease of life and literally set free. Filmed in key areas around the UK, the variety of locations gives the identity an inclusive feel, while the use of digital technology provides a filmic quality, which was both realistic and visually stunning, communicating the confidence and excellence of the programming. The pictured ident was used in 1997 and is no longer on air.

The BBC Two idents feature a '2' character who suffers different fates. The figure, personified as a robot, injected a sense of fun and mischief into the identity, allowing the channel to reach a younger and more urban target audience. This identity roll-out supported a scheduling change, which together attracted a new audience without alienating the existing viewers. This ident was used in 2001 and is no longer on air.

The BBC News ident features abstract globe imagery, conveying a sense of immediacy – a core value of any news service. Here, the globe is used as a constant device, but is presented in a rendered form, creating a different feel to the BBC One ident shown above. However, it still feels part of a 'family' and effectively slots in with the rest of the BBC idents. The three different idents demonstrate how a considered approach to design can create a dynamic and engaging set of visual pauses within a programming schedule, while maintaining a strong sense of cohesion, brand and identity. This is the BBC's current news ident.

Daniel Martin (right)

Pictured is the online portfolio created by UsLot Everywhere for international hairdressing salon Daniel Martin. It features simple imagery to show its capabilities, and no-nonsense messaging to direct users around the site.

Website design

Websites have become an integral visual communication tool for companies, organisations and individuals to communicate to their target audience. Websites can showcase products and services, and provide up-to-date information about news and events.

What is the point?

This is a question to bear in mind when developing a website as an online portfolio serves a different purpose from one presenting information and news events. Before beginning website development, it is important to define objectives and consider who the target audience is. How will the audience use the website? What message/information needs to be conveyed? Are there any technological requirements or constraints?

Who is the target audience?

The target audience influences all aspects of website design, from the presentation of information to navigation.

How will the audience use the website?

Clear navigation mechanisms need to exist within a site so it is important to bear in mind the experience and background of target users. The use of Internet search engines means users will not necessarily enter from the home page.

What is the message to be conveyed?

It is critical to define what you hope someone will remember after visiting a website. Be consistent and provide message elements on each page. If a company wants to project a sense of order and authority, then this must be conveyed in the page layout and structure.

Technological requirements / constraints

Technological restraints are often unseen until encountered and may not be straightforward to resolve. For example, some users may have older PC equipment and dial-up Internet access that cannot handle large, high-resolution graphics files, animations or other complex digital design elements.

Environmental design

——— Design in the environment includes informational and directional signage, exhibition space and outdoor media or advertising. It encompasses all design that exists within the built environment surrounding us. Although much of the design skill set is the same as for print and digital design, environmental design has some special considerations due to the different space and dimension the work has to function within.

Design and the human form

The principal difference in environmental design is that the relationship of a piece heavily relates to the human form. Environmental design tends to use a larger format and has to interact practically with physical structures. For instance, signage should be at eye level so that it is easily viewed.

The modernist architect Le Corbusier focused on the interaction between design and the human form in his piece *Le Modulor,* which he wrote between 1943 and 1955. It proposed a system of coordinated dimensions with which to design architecture based on the body dimensions of a six-foot English male.

Environmental design can subtly convey information or a mood, as seen in the examples on the opposite page, or in a more clear-cut way, such as directional signage.

The boundaries between these soft and hard approaches to communication in public spaces are breaking down as people grow accustomed to seeing ambient and direct messaging in public spaces. In essence, as people become more adept at picking out messages in the built environment, designers have greater flexibility to produce more subtle work.

Spaces not pages

Environmental design deals with spaces rather than pages. This means that a designer needs to consider how people interact with a space and its physical elements. Designing for a space is not dissimilar to designing for the printed page – in both cases the design tells a story, creates an impression, or a branded experience. However, spaces have obvious differences to pages due to the transition into the third dimension and the change of scale. For example, moving from the micro considerations of a typeset page to the macro considerations of interior or exterior spaces requires greater ability to imagine and conceptualise the final result.

Seven (above and right)

These interior wall murals were created by Studio Output
for the individually designed rooms of the boutique hotel,
Seven, in Bangkok, Thailand. The murals were inspired by
Thai culture and number cycles. The interior design was
developed around these concepts, providing a sense of
balance and harmony. The murals, created with a mixture of
raster and vector graphics, are integral to the environmental
experience of each room rather than being mere wall decoration
– they are mental shifts that represent a more profound,
unique and memorable graphic intervention.

Lily Nage

This brand identity was created by Research Studios for sportswear store Lily Nage and features a signage system with vibrant and attractive colours that work on many levels: there is directional signage (bottom right) and ambient signage (top right), where a quiet zone is created and occupied by the payment area. Iconic signage (bottom left) sees the image of a product reproduced on the wall with colours that are consistent with the overall store feel. Indicative images (top left) help shoppers find products for their sport of choice by focusing attention on the activity rather than the product. The use of scale makes the messages clear and accessible from a distance.

Signage and wayfinding

Design interventions in the physical environment include signage and wayfinding. Wayfinding is a visual key that allows people to navigate through a space by providing information to help them find their way around and work out how they can get to where they want to go. Signage incorporates all the visual information related to location and is the manifestation of wayfinding. It needs to be clear and easy to understand to be effective and therefore requires suitable aesthetics.

Signage and way finding interact in items such as maps. A shopping mall typically has maps on each floor that show the locations of different stores and food courts. Items such as the information desk, toilets, escalators, entrances and exits are often represented by symbols, which are also present on mall signage to help guide shoppers. The signage is a product of the way finding process.

Types of signs

There are many different signs and they fall into two basic categories: those we need to see (fire exits, evacuation routes and no-smoking signs), and those we want to see (toilets, escalators and where different stores are located). Signage uses colour and scale to differentiate between these two categories: the things we need to see tend to have a larger scale, be unequivocally coloured and placed in more prominent locations. Signage that guides us to other destinations may have a subtler scale and colouration.

Scale

Reading exhibition text involves moving one's head as well as one's eyes, and the need to be within visual range. Exhibitions benefit from concise, well-edited text bursts, rather than extended text blocks, with scale and quantity balanced. Small type sizes mean people need to be close to read them, and the possible need to wait. Large-format text can be read from anywhere in a room allows visitors to experience the event without necessarily peering at each exhibit description.

Screen design < **Environmental design** 129

signs and acrylic totems that stand 3.5 metres tall; the wayfinding hubs are positioned near the escalators to provide information so that customers can quickly orientate themselves. The combination of signage with location-specific information makes items accessible for both those people who are in a hurry and those with time to stop and study.

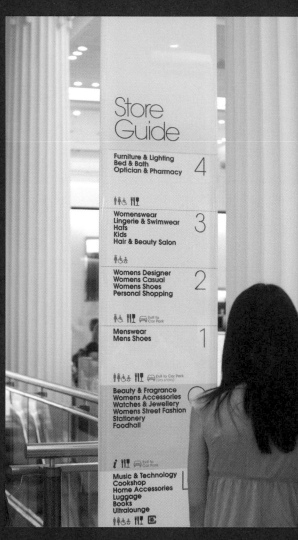

Barking Learning Centre
(left and below)

The signage for the Barking Learning Centre was created by Studio Myerscough. As with other communications developed for a company, signage not only tells us where to go, but it informs us about the organisation and speaks for the company. It conveys an organisation's aspirations and aims as part of its overall identity. In this example, the signage is very clear, precise and large, and sits comfortably with the purpose of a learning establishment.

National Portrait Gallery (right)

These posters by NB: Studio use a standard format that provides a large space for a design to be eye-catching when displayed outdoors. While the text cannot be read at a distance, the eyes in both portraits are positioned in line with the rule of thirds, which engage the interest of the viewer.

 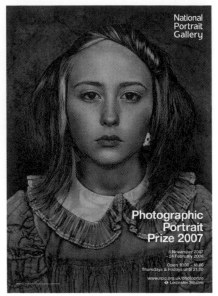

Outdoor media

Signage appears in a variety of outdoor media such as billboards and the sides of buses, trains and taxi cabs. Each different media presents its own design challenges in terms of scale and exposure time.

Scale

Outdoor media has a wide range of scales – from the relatively small size of a taxi cab to a 48-panel billboard (or larger). The scale of the active area affects the amount and size of content that will be displayed on it. A large billboard should not contain a great deal of detail in small text as it is unlikely that the audience will be able to get close enough to read it. Large billboards are meant to make a big impression that people can see from a distance.

Exposure time

Not all outdoor media is stationary and this means they may be exposed to viewers for a limited time. When a communication is to be displayed as mobile media, such as a poster on a bus or taxi, it should focus on creating a memorable impression rather than providing extensive detailed information. For these reasons, outdoor media designs tend to include a striking image, minimal text and perhaps just a brand and slogan. This also holds for fixed media where people are likely to be mobile, such as posters displayed in train stations and along roadsides. In locations where people will be stationary, there will be increased exposure time, and this allows for the inclusion of more detailed information. Many advertisements inside urban transport systems feature detailed texts as passengers will have the time and inclination to read them on their journey.

pobl + machines
(right and above)

Why Not Associates collaborated with artist Gordon Young to create this outdoor installation for the National Waterfront Museum in Swansea. The design features letter-shaped seats that chart the industrial heritage of Wales and spell 'pobl', which means 'people' in Welsh. Each letter also represents a machine or an item on display in the museum, highlighting that outdoor media encompasses more than the traditional billboard.

Design Now Austria (right)

The installation in this example uses scale and curved forms to interact with space and guide people around it. It was created for the exhibition Design Now Austria by Büro X.

Exhibition design

Exhibition design is about engaging someone within a three-dimensional environment rather than providing a static display of well-ordered artefacts. Interactivity, marketing material support, websites, narrative and structure all contribute to a more rounded and balanced approach to exhibition design that is more appealing to the public, facilitating the educational process and transfer of knowledge. Both exhibition and print-design planning start with clear objectives about the information to be presented and what the key messages are, conveyed via a linear narrative to maintain a certain pace and intensity.

Exhibitions are not books on walls

An exhibition is typically accompanied by supporting print material in addition to the text presented in the physical environment. It is unrealistic to expect the audience to absorb information as they would when reading a book as an exhibition hall has distractions (movement from other visitors or noise), making it difficult to concentrate. Heavy editing of material is required to distil the message into a form that can be transformed into an easily understandable and digestible visual experience.

Designers work with a <u>curator</u> who determines exhibition content, develops the key themes and formulates the sequence. A designer interprets and visualises these ideas and organises them into a coherent and functional three-dimensional space, with appropriate signage.

Curators

When creating an exhibition space, a designer often has to work with the curator programming the exhibition material. A curator determines the content of the exhibition, develops the key themes and formulates its order or sequence. Once all the material has been decided, it is then the designer's job to interpret and visualise these ideas and organise it into a coherent and functional three-dimensional space, using appropriate signage.

London Open City (left and below)

The London Open City exhibition at Somerset House, London and Bucharest was jointly designed by Studio Myerscough and Gerrard O'Carroll for Design for London. Notice how internal and external spaces are used together with changing scales and the unexpected. The telescopes had pre-recorded panoramic videos of London.

Retail design

The design of the retail environment has both practical and aesthetic considerations that combine to create an atmosphere in which customers will buy products. At a practical level, retail design has to allow customers to see, and possibly touch, the merchandise. However, it also needs to visually present items in such a way as to appear attractive and desirable. This often entails creating an environment that resembles the aspirations of the consumer, or one that reflects the conditions in which the merchandise will be used. As such, retail design is the translation of <u>brand values</u> into the built environment.

As buyers become more sophisticated, they are better able to see through contrived presentations and so retail design continues to evolve to meet the needs and demands of increasingly savvy shoppers.

Oliver Spencer

The images on this spread show the identity and retail environment created by Marque for the Oliver Spencer clothing store. The retail environment has a homely feel that is eclectic and unconventional; it was created through the use of the collection of objects that sets a scene and allows a customer to feel as though they are browsing through an old house filled with intriguing items. The logotype is a re-cut typewriter font inspired by a pre-school, utilitarian explorer aesthetic.

Brand values

Attributes that convey the essence and core beliefs brand, such as excellence, quality and integrity.

Chapter 5
Procuring work

It is ironic that many graphic designers, in spite of being responsible for creating attractive, memorable and even iconographic images to promote their clients, often struggle when it comes to their own self-promotion. Considered, thoughtful and targeted self-promotion is the designer's key to obtaining regular work. Successful graphic design, like any creative industry, has to be underpinned by a solid economic platform.

Self-promotion is an integral part of the work of any graphic designer, whether an individual practitioner or a member of a thriving design agency. This chapter outlines some of the key considerations to promote your design business.

Marque website (opposite)

This is the website of design studio Marque, formerly Third Eye Design. The site ingeniously reorders the sample thumbnail images to fit the browser width of each viewer. The design is made informative and engaging through the use of animation. It adds interest without being distracting and viewers quickly gain an overview of the site's contents. The inclusion of a client zone and other features makes the site well-rounded and robust.

Marque

Newsletter
Client Login
Search

Recent Projects

Begg
The Chicago Spire
The Common Guild
Dow Jones
Edinburgh Festival Fringe
For One More Day
Kshocolat
The Macallan
Archive Projects
News
Clients
Contact

Overview

Begg are recognised as the manufacturer of the finest cashmere accessories in the world. Based in Ayrshire, Scotland, they are renowned in the textile industry for producing a unique cashmere material using a combination of contemporary design coupled with technology, craft and process that dates back many hundreds of years. Unsurprisingly, their clients include other 'Craft Houses' such as Hermes and Louis Vuitton.

In recent years however Begg has been faced with an interesting and familiar problem. With the demise of the Multi Fibre trade agreement, countries with a large cheaper labour forces have been handed the potential to dominate the textile industry.

In response to this and in order to sustain growth, Begg have devised a strategy to strengthen its own brand. With this in mind, Marque was brought on board to help launch Begg own branded products. The result is a perfect combination of craft and dynamism, evoking the spirit of the brand – the identity evolving into a beautiful array of foil blocks, die stamps and textured paper stocks – the photography and art direction looking at the cashmere as art.

Related Links:
www.beggscotland.com

Self-promotion

———— Graphic designers obtain the bulk of their commissions through self-promotion. Successful self-promotion starts with undertaking adequate research about a client or agency; a designer must find out as much as possible regarding the nature of their prospective client's business and the key contacts within the company. The following lists the avenues available for self-promotion.

First impressions

First impressions count for a lot so ensure that all information is correct – the names of the people holding your future earning potential in their hands must be spelt correctly on any communication. Once sent, always make a follow-up call.

Promotion should not be restricted to potential clients who you know of. There are various means to cast the net further and promote yourself to potential clients you may not have heard of by submitting work to magazines and journals. All of the work contained in this book and the others in AVA's Basics Design series serve to promote the creative abilities of various contributors and design studios.

Submissions for self-promotion must follow the same basic principles as pitching to clients: they must be well-targeted and include details of who it was produced for, so that the writer or journalist writing the piece can refer to a full body of information. Magazines regularly receive samples of work and have limited time available, so it is useful to submit samples of work where information is readily visible and available.

Printed mailers

Printed mailers allow a design studio to show existing and potential clients some of their design, format section and print finishing capabilities. In the digital age, there is still immense value in producing physical pieces that present a permanent and more memorable message.

Printed mailers allow designers to place a physical piece of work in the hands of potential clients, enabling them to feel the tactile qualities of a piece through the careful selection of stock, printing and print-finishing processes. However, the production of mailers brings with it practical considerations such as format selection, print run, printing and postage costs.

Mailers must be correctly and clearly addressed, with the name of the recipient and their company spelt correctly, and your own contact details easy to locate. Instead of waiting for a potential client to call, it is good practice to make a follow-up call after a mailer has been sent out.

The Vast Agency (left)

This broadsheet loose-leaf mailer was created by The Vast Agency to demonstrate the talents of the group and the photographers and stylists who they work with. Producing a mailer is a subtle way to procure work – it shows what an agency is capable of rather than directly trying to sell its services to a potential client.

James Brown (below)

These pieces are from a pack of A6 postcards created by illustrator James Brown, who works under the moniker of General Pattern. The cards reflect this name and show the diversity of his work. The postcards are tactile and memorable, but their size gives them a familiarity that prevents them from appearing flashy; they also invite the viewer to view his website: www.generalpattern.net.

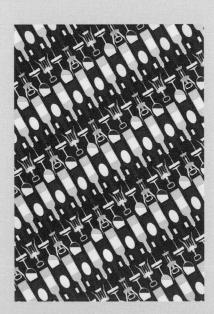

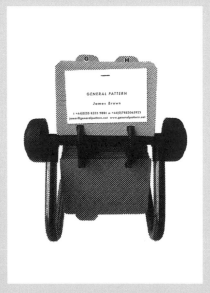

We are Them®

Our work
  Rebranding
  New Brands
  Print
    AOP
    British Heart Foundation
    Borkowski Christmas Card
    FACT Magazine
    Getty Images
    Hammerson
    Jones Lang LaSalle
    Westbury Hotel
    Warner Brothers
  Editorial
  Books
  Music
  Online
  Film
Our clients
The way we work
Contact us

Them (right)

Pictured are images from a website created by and for design studio Them, which showcases their work and underlines how integral online portfolios have become to the marketing effort of such companies.

Designer websites

Websites have become an integral visual communication tool for designers and design studios alike. They showcase work to other studios and prospective clients, while also providing inspiration.

Websites for design studios are typically directed towards showing examples of work to a very specific group of users, such as advertising agencies, marketing departments or other creatives. Websites are used to present an online portfolio showing examples of the creative approaches a studio has and the different media and sectors it typically works in. Visual information and text provide details that support the examples in the portfolio, such as the client, the format a work was produced in, and the contact details of the studio. Before beginning website development, it is important to create a list of site considerations, which may include:

1 Who is the target audience?
2 How will the target audience use the site?
3 What is the message?
4 Are there any technological requirements and constraints?

A clear navigation mechanism needs to exist within a site. Its complexity should match the experience and background of its target users. A design studio may present its portfolio by client, sector or media using a flat structure so that there aren't too many levels to click through.

Design studio websites tend to showcase work in a way that allows prospective clients to obtain a clear understanding of their capabilities and the different media used. While most visitors to a design website are likely to be viewing it on equipment that can handle complex graphics and animation, this may not always be the case.

Shufti (left and below)

The digital showreel below was created by The Vast Agency to promote its talents and those of its designers and photographers. This studio specialises in work for the fashion industry, hence its target audience is familiar with fashion magazines. This showreel takes the familiar format further by creating magazines with different contents and themes. The magazine is also printed for distribution and pictured here are pages from three issues: Sex in the City, Sunstroke, and Rendezvous.

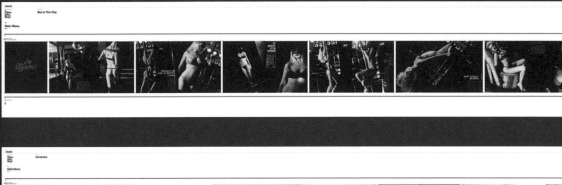

Studio Output (left)

This HTML email from Studio Output allows the recipient to click on any section to access the relevant page of the company's website. The visual qualities of HTML email provide a clear statement of the sender's activities that in this instance are clearly composed, colour-coded sections that aid navigation. This type of communication now forms an integral part of the marketing and publicity strategies of many companies.

Types of electronic communications

Electronic communications, such as a website or CD-ROM, are used by design agencies to provide information about themselves to both prospective and existing clients. They also provide a platform to showcase their work, expertise and creativity.

Designers traditionally showcased their work through printed pieces, but the development of digital media has allowed them to branch out and extend the scope of their promotional efforts. Digital and print media provide different costs and benefits: digital may not be tactile, but it is immediate, has low distribution costs and can reach more people. The work samples showcased can also be updated easily and regularly.

The development of email and Internet technology means that people have migrated from emailing a file to sending an HTML email containing codes to access files that are stored externally rather than included in the email. This reduces message sizes and prevents communication from being blocked by computer firewalls.

The increasing popularity of blogging provides another promotional avenue as a design studio can communicate about its current activities and receive comments and feedback from viewers.

PDF mail shots

These are image files sent as PDFs, allowing people to view work. However, they can result in large file sizes.

HTML mailers

This format is a smaller file size for email; images are stored externally and accessed by an HTML link. This means that the communication is not blocked by computer protection software. It is considered good practice to allow people to opt out of receiving these emails.

CDs/DVDs

These methods of electronic storage and transport are bulky and have higher distribution costs than email as they need to be sent by post.

Blogs

This type of electronic communication provides the opportunity to communicate regularly and informally with the target audience.

Agency communication path to clients

Off-page activity

Agency website → Client

On-page activity

Client's communication path to design agency

Client → Agency

This diagram shows the communication flow between agencies and clients.

Closing the loop

There are many ways of developing and presenting a website, but the key factor is its focal point. There are two website types that design agencies use: an online portfolio and an online blog.

A portfolio website sees text and images from completed projects presented as a series of examples to show the skills and depth of knowledge of the agency. These are usually divided into subcategories such as print, online, exhibition, corporate, fashion, etc. As with a physical portfolio, good housekeeping is necessary – edit the number of pieces shown so that you cover all creative bases without being overwhelming.

A blog allows the designers to add thoughts, inspirations and stories to the work shown and provides an insight into how design decisions were made and arrived at. This approach requires comments to be updated, and kept fresh and current, necessitating an ongoing time commitment that a portfolio website does not.

The illustration above shows how on-page and off-page marketing activities are used to enhance the performance and effectiveness of a website. An agency will usually email or send printed items to prospective clients containing web address details in an attempt to link them back to the website to close the loop. Sending regular HTML emails or marketing material ensures that this relationship stays active, which means that new material needs to be developed to stay fresh.

On-page marketing
Optimises the communication effectiveness of a webpage, such as keyword activity.
Off-page marketing
This includes blogs, news sections and HTML emails which serve as communication vehicles to distribute a message.

Portfolios

—— A portfolio is a collection of the best pieces of work by a designer and is used to showcase their abilities and special talents to prospective clients. The effectiveness of a portfolio depends on how it is presented and the careful selection of the work it contains.

Portfolios – things to consider

Recent graduates and seasoned designers alike use their portfolio as a means of generating work. All portfolios serve more or less the same purpose: they are essentially a carrying device that holds samples of work showing what the designer is capable of. However, there are other considerations that may affect how successfully a portfolio will present the work it holds.

Size

The large portfolios typically used by design students are too big for general everyday purposes. Graduates quickly learn this after spending a week walking the streets with an object that is almost as big, and possibly just as heavy, as they are. It is important to consider where and how a portfolio will be shown to prospective clients. Most interviews are conducted at a desk, so a practically sized portfolio may be more reasonable and efficient to use.

Order

A portfolio is a series of bound leaves that forms a sequential order, and this order creates a narrative, whether intentional or not. A bound portfolio means that a designer is locked into the order of the work, which may result in a lot of flicking back and forth to locate specific work examples. If the leaves are unbound, the relevant examples can be easily removed and shown to the client.

Sifer Design portfolio

A bound portfolio lends a solid and professional feel to the work it contains and often gives a better visual impression than a loose-leaf box portfolio. A bound portfolio gives a designer less flexibility to rearrange and change work samples, whereas a loose-leaf portfolio provides more flexibility – the content and order can be tailored to each prospective client. More expensive portfolios feature transparent sleeves made from an anti-glare material that ensure optimum optical viewing quality.

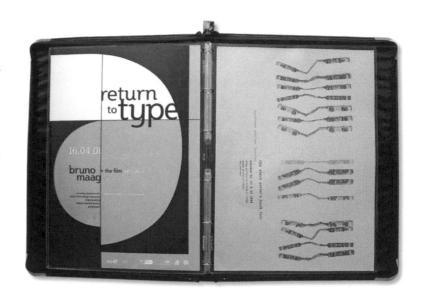

Quantity and selection

A loose-leaf portfolio also has the advantage of allowing the content to be tailored to the needs, style and speciality of a specific client or interview. It also allows for new work to be included, which helps to maintain a designer's own interest as well as that of an interviewer. A designer needs to carefully consider the range of pieces that will be showcased in a portfolio. Work that is too similar may give the impression that the designer has a limited range of abilities; too broad and it may be difficult for the client to form a definite opinion about their suitability for a job.

The quantity of work shown is also important. Designers have a tendency to show too much work rather than applying the principle of <u>Ockham's razor</u> – pare down to the best pieces, but maintain variety. Include a print piece, a website and an identity. A range between five and ten pieces is enough to convey a sense of passion and self belief, while keeping the interest of the interviewer.

Your 'book'

Portfolios are often requested by clients without the designer being present, which means that when you drop your 'book' off at an advertising agency, it needs to make the right impression. The sequence needs to be easy to understand and it must have an accessible narrative. An electronic PDF version should be given to the potential client on a memory stick or CD-ROM.

The format of the portfolio is also an important consideration. Low-quality portfolios have reflective sleeves that cause glare and impede viewing. High-end portfolios are more expensive, but have reduced-glare sleeves and often come in more presentable boxes or folders. Some designers also have boxes that are custom-made to present their portfolios – these further project their personality and creative skills.

Ockham's razor

A principle attributed to the fourteenth-century English logician and Franciscan friar, William of Ockham, which forms the basis of methodological reductionism in that elements that are not really needed should be pared back to produce something simpler.

Chapter 6
The production process

_____ This final chapter looks at the basic tool kit a graphic designer uses to create and produce effective designs. The tools unleash and channel creative ideas from the design process into workable and physical products – through the printing process or for electronic applications such as web pages. This section also includes basic information on how to ensure that control is maintained over the use of images and colour.

In-Cosmetics (opposite)

This brochure created by Research Studios helps to establish a visual identity and platform for cosmetics innovation. The use of a colourful, dreamy image alludes to how cosmetics provide a wealth of possibilities, which interact to improve the appearance of the people using them. The fine detail and the importance of image quality to the business of the client meant that high-end filled paper stock with excellent printability and colour-reception characteristics had to be used. In this example, minimal dot gain is vital to avoid registration problems. High opacity and whiteness are necessary to provide a crisp, clean background that allow the colours to reproduce as intended.

Areas looked at in this chapter

...and enhance sex appeal.

Sex Appeal plant extracts by Greentech:

Pomegranate (Punica granatum)
Throughout history the pomegranate, associated with Aphrodite, has been the symbol of fertility and the focus of legends of love. It is specifically mentioned in the Kama Sutra as a valuable aid in lovemaking. In ancient Greece the pomegranate was the symbol of Dionysian rites.

Saffron (Crocus sativus)
It was praised in ancient China as sexual stimulant. In Rome the plant was dedicated to Ceres the Goddess of Fertility. Pliny recommended it to inspire love games.

Pepper (Capsicum pepper)
The irreplaceable ingredient of love rituals, the vegetable with a suggestive shape instills burning desire.

Basic tools

——— Designers have access to various traditional and modern tools that provide great flexibility in the design process and the work that results. From hands-on craft-based tools, such as a scalpel and cutting mat, to a personal computer with a drawing tablet, designers can express themselves in any number of ways to experiment and develop a visual idea.

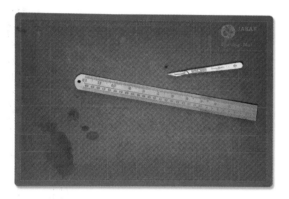

Cutting mat (above)

A good quality, rubber cutting mat should be used with a scalpel to stop the blade from sliding; the rubber mat protects both the scalpel handler and desk surfaces. Available in rubber or composite vinyl materials, cutting mats often include grid patterns and angle guidelines to help make precisely measured cuts. The compacted nature of the mat material means that they self-repair and maintain a smooth surface that does not show cutting lines or marks.

Scalpel (above)

A scalpel is a blade used for cutting stock – an essential tool for the creation of dummies and mock-ups. Scalpels are available with a range of different handles and interchangeable blades, which should be changed regularly to ensure optimum performance. Cutting should be performed so that you cut-to-waste – the cut is made through the waste stock being cut away and not the printed item that will be the product.

Cutting rule (above)

A cutting rule is a metal ruler that is used to make cuts of accurate length. Metal is used rather than plastic as the latter material is easily nicked by the blade, which alters and distorts the straight edge. Cutting rules can be flat or have a raised profile to help keep the cutter's fingers away from the blade.

Spray mount (above)

Spray mount is an aerosol adhesive used to bond two or more pieces of stock together for the production of mock-ups and dummies. There are several types available: the basic spray mount is used for producing mock-ups; the display mount provides a more permanent bond; and low-tack adhesives allow for repositioning. Spray mount should ideally be used in a spray booth or a separate, well-ventilated area in order to prevent sticky adhesive residue being applied to the face side of any prints.

Loupe (above)

A loupe is a magnifying lens used to check proofs and transparencies. Photographer's loupes offer 8x magnification, while printer's loupes offer 10x or 14x magnification.

Protractor (above)

A protractor is a semi-circular tool used to measure angles.

Writing ink (above)

Writing ink is a pigment-containing liquid deposited on to paper by a pen or brush. When used for lettering, it can add a vernacular element and immediacy that printed letter forms cannot.

Watercolour and brushes (above)

Watercolour is a paint that has water-soluble pigment, which allows its colours to be diluted. Designers apply watercolour in thumbnail sketches as flood colour to rapidly cover large areas.

Marker pens (above)

Marker pens have their own supply of ink that is deposited on to the stock through a porous tip. Pens are available with different tip shapes although they will commonly have a fine and a thin edge.

Fine line pens (above)

Fine line pens that produce various line weights are available. They start from 0.25mm and get progressively thicker to provide for different drawing and sketching needs. Desktop publishing and drawing packages have also adopted these line weights.

Tapes (above)

Designers use different types of adhesive tape for different jobs, such as to mask parts of a design; to fix work to a board; or to temporarily hold structures together.

Roller (above)

A roller is used in conjunction with a cutting mat and an adhesive for pressing together different sheets of stock to form backed-up prints that are used for dummies.

Scale rule (above)

Scale rules have a measurement scale that present different ratios as a fraction of an inch or millimetre. A common sight in architectural practices, such rules offer scales such as 1:16, 1:32 and 1:64. These rules are invaluable for a designer producing work for an exhibition, signage or environmental design.

Type scale (below)

A type scale is a rule that measures in points (the basic unit used for type), as well as millimetres. Designers may use a type scale when sketching out a layout to insert type of an approximate size.

French curves (below)

A French curve is a drafting tool used to produce smoothly drawn curves.

Digital media (below)

Digital files can be stored on a range of different media. CDs and DVDs are relatively cheap ways of storing, sending and viewing digital information. Memory sticks or pen drives are a highly portable and reusable means of storing digital files.

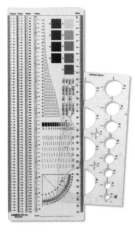

Paper (below)

A multitude of different papers are available to the designer including tracing paper, watercolour paper that does not crinkle when wet, and sturdy cartridge paper.

Pencils (below)

Pencils contain a graphite core that is used to leave a mark on paper. The intensity of the mark depends on the hardness or softness of the graphite. This is represented by the HB classification system in the UK, ranging from 9B (softest and darkest) to 9H (hardest and lightest). US writing pencils have a number system in which #1 is a B grade, #2 is HB, #3 is H and #4 is 2H.

Stencils (below)

A stencil is a template of holes that form letters and numbers, which can be drawn through and on to a substrate with a pen.

Drawing tablet (above)

An electronic tablet is drawn upon with a stylus and acts as an interface between the designer and the computer. This offers the freedom of freehand drafting, using different tools for rapid production and editing of drawn images.

Scanner (above)

A device that produces an electronic file by scanning artwork or an image with a battery of electronic sensors thus recording information.

Printer (above)

A printer is a device used to deposit ink on to a substrate. Many types of printers are available – from desktop inkjet to laser printers. They can produce four-colour work at varying speeds and qualities.

Letraset (below)

Letraset are transfers of typographical characters available in a wide range of fonts. They were a key design tool for producing mock-ups before the benefits of desktop computing became available.

Software (below)

A computer program that enables the user to operate and perform specific functions on a computer and related devices, such as scanners and printers.

Printing papers (below)

Printing papers are various speciality papers that designers use when mounting presentations. Examples include gloss, double sided and matt.

Pantone swatches (right and below right)

Pantone swatches are essential to obtain accurate colour printing. Several different swatch books are available, which correspond to different collections of Pantone colours, such as the spot, metallic and pastel swatches shown here. The Pantone system allocates a letter and a number to each colour. Some colours may also be named. The equivalent CMYK colour swatches show how Pantone colours reproduce using the CMYK printing process. Swatches allow a designer to see colour discrepancies at the design stage rather than when a job is on the press.

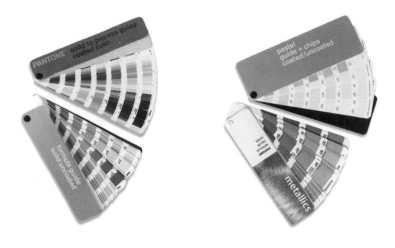

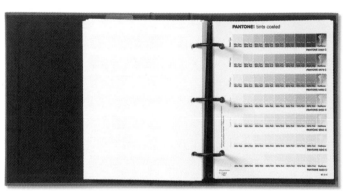

Typeface samplers (left)

A typeface sampler is a swatch book for fonts, which allows a designer to consider a wider range when selecting letterforms for a job.

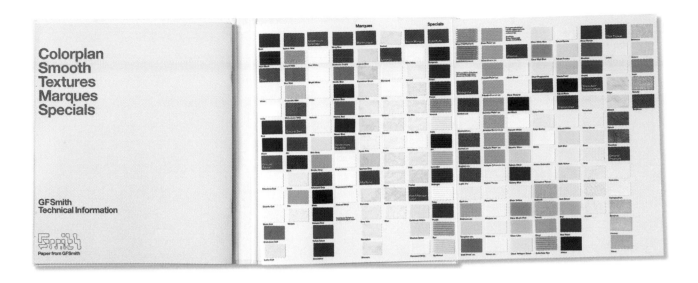

Colorplan
Smooth
Textures
Marques
Specials

GFSmith
Technical Information

Paper from GFSmith

Paper swatches (above, right and below)

Most designers keep paper swatches containing samples of different stocks for reference and inspiration.

A paper swatch contains examples of different types of stock allowing a designer to assess the appropriateness of their visual and tactile qualities for a job. Most stock suppliers produce swatches that can be requested and obtained free of charge.

Specialist colour

———— Colour is a crucial part of graphic design today, but it is something that consumers, clients and designers take for granted. Colour can bring a design to life, help to establish hierarchies, highlight key information and add pace and emotion to a design. However, it is a design aspect that is easy to get wrong and causes problems when a job prints incorrectly.

Getting colour right

Colour control is one of the primary tasks that a graphic designer is responsible for in the print production process. This is achieved through colour management, a process that governs how colour is translated from one piece of equipment to another (for instance, from digital camera to a computer to the printing press), ensuring accurate and predictable colour reproduction. Colour management is needed because each device responds to and produces colour differently.

Colour spaces

Designers can work with different colour spaces – systems that define the hue, saturation and value of a colour in the different design and printing processes. Colour spaces include RGB (red, green, blue) and CMYK (cyan, magenta, yellow and black), which are used by colour monitors and the four-colour printing process. However, there are other colour spaces, such as the six-colour Hexachrome printing process and the 16-bit system that stores colour information and yields over 65,000 colours.

RGB/CMYK

A colour is made up of different quantities of red, green and blue light, which can be presented as a ratio. These ratios produce different results in different colour spaces. RGB is the additive primary colour space that computer monitors use and CMYK is the subtractive primary colour space used in the four-colour printing process. In order to achieve accurate and reliable colour reproduction, it is necessary to know how the different devices in the design and print production system use colour.

Red, green and blue (RGB) are the additive primaries that form white light, and they are used to produce colour images on a computer screen. The RGB colour space that computer monitors use can reproduce about 70 per cent of the colours of the spectral gamut that can be perceived by the human eye. Cyan, magenta, yellow and black (CMYK) are the subtractive primaries used in the four-colour printing process where each represents one of the print colours. Computer images in the RGB colour space are converted to the CYMK colour space for printing.

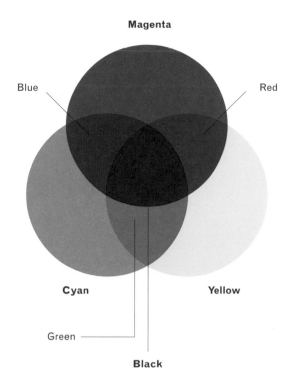

Magenta

Blue — Red

Cyan — Yellow

Green

Black

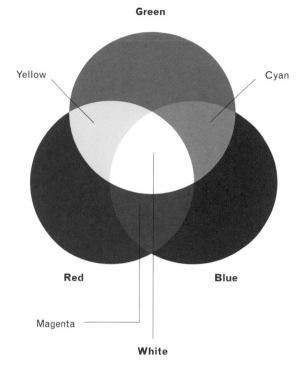

Green

Yellow — Cyan

Red — Blue

Magenta

White

Subtractive primaries (above)

Each subtractive primary is formed from two of the additive primary colours as shown above. Where two subtractive primaries overlap, they create an additive primary colour.

Additive primaries (above)

Additive primary colours represent a component of white light. Where two additive primaries overlap, they create a subtractive primary colour.

Describing colour

Every colour corresponds to a unique wavelength of light, but to communicate better concepts of colour, a simple method of describing it has developed to make things easier. Colour can be described according to three features: its hue or colour; its saturation or chroma; and its value or brightness.

Hue

Hue refers to the unique characteristic of a colour that helps us visually distinguish one colour from another. Hues or colours are formed by different wavelengths of light.

Saturation

Saturation or chroma refers to the purity of a colour and saturation levels describe a colour's tendency to move towards or away from grey.

Brightness

Brightness or value refers to how light or dark a colour is. Changes in the brightness value can be achieved by mixing a colour with black or white.

Various business cards by Parent Design (above)

These business cards by Parent Design are for different clients. Each card features the use of a different colour stock and silver foil-blocked text. The different colours alter our perception and feeling towards the companies as they have various cognitive meanings, such as pink for girls and blue for boys. Black gives a serious appearance; white has a clean and pure aspect; and the reddish pink is playful. Careful colour selection is crucial to avoid unwanted interpretations.

Colour calibration

Calibration is a process whereby the colour space of a monitor or other piece of equipment is adjusted to be equal to that of a given standard. For example, sRGB (standard RGB) is a device-independent, calibrated colour space defined by Hewlett Packard and Microsoft in the 1990s to provide a consistent way to display colour Internet images on computer screens.

Pantone system

The Pantone PMS colour system is one that covers a wide range of different hues, including special, metallic and pastel colours. The Pantone system allocates a unique reference number to each hue and shade to facilitate communication between designers and printers, and to ensure that specific colours are used in a design. Monitors can be calibrated to the Pantone system so that on-screen colours match those in the swatch books.

Monitor

A monitor or screen is a device used to produce images using red, green and blue light. However, monitors need to be calibrated so that they display colours as they would print on an output device.

Printer

Different printing devices use different inks, which means that a job will print with slightly different colours depending on the device it is output on. An inkjet will produce different results to a four-colour litho press, which will again differ in result from a six-colour litho press. For this reason, it is necessary to consider how a design will be output so that the colours reproduce as intended.

Websafe colours

Websafe colours are a group of 216 colours considered to be safe for use in the design of web pages. This palette came into being when computer monitors were only able to display 256 colours and were chosen to match the colour palettes of leading web browsers of the time. The websafe colour palette allows for the production of six shades of red, green and blue. This palette has the highest number of distinct colours within which each colour group can be distinguished individually.

Monitor

This is the device upon which a design is viewed. It must be colour calibrated to give an accurate representation of the colours that will reproduce in print.

Spyder

This is a colour calibration system for monitors and printers. A monitor is calibrated so that a designer has an accurate idea of how colours will appear when a job is printed.

External storage

As artwork, images and photos tend to be large files that take up a lot of storage space, external hard drives are useful for keeping the main workstation unclogged, in addition to providing a means of backing-up work.

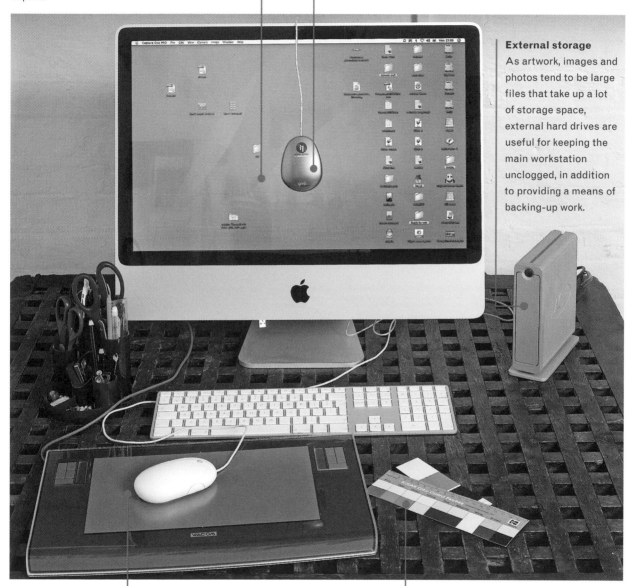

Tablet

A drawing tablet gives a designer the ability to draw freehand images directly on to the computer screen.

Colour control patch

This provides a means of maintaining colour consistency In photographed images.

File formats

—— Designers have to work with different electronic image types that are stored in different formats due to the various kinds of images and how they will be used. Digital images can be stored in several ways, each of which has advantages and disadvantages that a graphic designer needs to understand.

Image types

The two main image types are raster (bitmap) and vector (line art). A raster image is one that is composed of pixels in a grid, where each pixel contains colour information for the reproduction of the image. Rasters have a fixed resolution, which means that an enlargement of the image results in a decrease in quality.

On the other hand, a vector image contains many scalable objects that are defined by mathematical formulae, or paths, rather than pixels. Vectors are therefore scalable and resolution-independent. They can be enlarged infinitely and will remain crisp and clear. Vectors are used for storing logos as they have no background colour, which means they can be placed over other artwork.

These sunflowers are raster images. Notice how the detail shows that the image is made up of individual pixels.

These designs are vector images that contain many individual and scalable objects defined by mathematical formulae, which means they are resolution independent.

Orange Life (right)

These images from *Orange Life* magazine were created by Vault 49 and features a mixture of different image types. The photograph is a raster (normally saved as a TIFF), while the illustrations are vector graphics that are in EPS format. The resulting image is a combination of the two file types.

Main file formats

There are four main digital image file formats: TIFF (Tagged Image File Format), JPEG (Joint Photographic Experts Group), GIF (Graphic Interchange Format) and EPS (Encapsulated PostScript).

TIFFs are mainly used for print. The JPEG file format is used for print as well for screen applications, such as websites. GIFs are for screen use, including animation. Lastly, the EPS file format is used to save multi-channel images from Photoshop, such as duotones and clipping paths (which are not scalable) and for vector graphics that are scalable.

Vector files must be saved as EPS to retain their scalability. This format is used for corporate logos as they are easily portable and self-contained, which means they cannot be altered from within desktop publishing programs.

Format	Advantages	Uses
Bitmap	Image constructed by fixed number of pixels that are easily coloured.	Continuous tone images, tonal images.
TIFF	A flexible, cross-platform compatible format that retains high image quality suitable for printing.	Halftones and colour images.
JPEG	24-bit colour information (6.7 million colours); uses compression to reduce file size.	Images with complex pixel gradations and continuous tone.
EPS	Files can be resided, distorted and colour separated.	Storing vector or object-based artwork.
PSD	Versatile format that supports all available image modes (bitmap, grayscale, duotone, RGB, CMYK etc).	Producing and working on images prior to conversion to final format.

Print finishing

—— Print finishing encompasses a range of processes that are used to provide the final touches to a job – it can transform an ordinary-looking piece into something much more spectacular. These processes may include die-cutting, embossing, debossing, foil-blocking, varnishing and screen-printing.

Print-finishing considerations

Print-finishing processes add the final touches to a printed piece. This can include decorative elements such as the shimmer of a foil block or the texture provided by an emboss or screen print, in addition to added functionality, such as the protective nature of a varnish or something that is fundamental to the format, such as a binding. For example, a die cut removes part of the substrate and can be used to change the shape of the piece, or to provide an aperture through which other parts of the publication may be viewed.

Print-finishing processes may be performed online as the substrate comes off the printing press (online varnish), or offline as a separate operation once printing is completed (foil block).

Print-finishing processes have the ability to dramatically enhance a job, and although they represent the end of the production process, they should be considered as an integral part of the design and not as an afterthought once a piece has been printed. The successful use of print finishing techniques means their application must be planned as part of the initial design to maximise the benefits derived and to control costs.

Binding

Binding is a collective term for a range of processes used to hold together the pages or sections of a publication to form a book, magazine, brochure or other printed product. The different binding methods available allow a designer to make choices about the functionality as well as the visual qualities, longevity and cost of a publication. Used creatively, binding can provide a simple means of differentiating a publication. Options include perfect binding, sewn or burst binding, and saddle-stitching.

Moot

This folder contains eight A5 artist postcards created by Studio Output for the Zoo Art Fair 07. It uses a black rubber band as a binding and a silver foil block on a micron cover. The binding method allows the content to be held together as one unit, but also means they can be separated into independent and autonomous pieces.

51° 48° – 04° 40° (above, right and below)
This catalogue by Faydherbe / De Vringer takes the form of a screen-printed, linen-covered box containing loose, printed pieces that was created to hold various art projects. As some were not ready when the project was under development, a conventional bound catalogue could not be produced. The printed pieces are printed on contrasting glossy and uncoated stocks.

Types of binding

Perfect binding

Binding where the backs of sections are removed and held together with a flexible adhesive, which also attaches a paper cover to the spine, and the fore edge is trimmed flat.

Case or edition binding

This is commonly used for hard cover books. It sews signatures together, flattens the spine, applies endpapers and head and tail bands to the spine. Hard covers are attached and grooves along the cover edge act as hinges.

Canadian

A wiro-bound publication with a wrap-around cover and an enclosed spine. A complete wrap-around cover is a full Canadian and a partial wraparound is a half Canadian.

Comb and spiral binding

Comb binding uses plastic (comb) rings that allow a document to open flat. Spiral binding uses metal wire that winds through punched holes in the stock, which allows the publication to open flat.

Open bind

A book bound without a cover, leaving an exposed spine.

Belly band

A printed band that wraps around a publication, typically used with magazines.

Saddle stitch

Signatures are nested and bound with wire stitches applied through the spine along the centrefold.

Singer stitch

A binding method where pages are sewn together with one continual thread.

Clips and bolts

A fastening device that holds loose pages together. This usually requires the insertion of a punched or drilled hole for the bolt or clip to pass through.

Paper engineering

Paper engineering refers to the various methods by which paper stock can be manipulated and formed during print finishing including folding, die-cutting and perforating to produce specific formats or decorative effects.

Hans van Bentem (above and right)

This combination of folder, postcards and booklet celebrate the opening of the Dutch Embassy's new building in South Africa. It showcases the art produced by Hans van Bentem. The postcards feature sculptures produced after the rest of the job was printed. The artist took photographs of the sculptures the day before the opening, which were processed at a nearby photo lab and then added to the printed folders. This piece was designed by Faydherbe / De Vringer.

Gordon Russell Museum, Vision and Reality (above)

This commemorative brochure by Webb & Webb showcases the beautiful detailing of Sir Gordon Russell's furniture on the cover. The book flaps create a facsimile of cupboard doors that open and function like a trompe l'oeil, while the endpapers show a cabinet interior.

Corbis (below)

This foldout pamphlet by Jog Design reveals information sequentially as the item is unfolded before finally showing the full design.

Printing

Printing encompasses a range of direct and indirect methods for transferring an ink on to a substrate, including lithography, screen-printing, intaglio or gravure.

Printing methods

Lithography
The inked image from a printing plate is transferred or offset on to a rubber blanket roller that is then pressed against the substrate. Lithography uses a smooth printing plate and functions on the basis that oil and water repel each other.

Web printing
This uses stock that is supplied on large rolls rather than individual sheets. It allows for higher printing speeds, higher volumes and lower production costs per unit. Webs can be used with lithography and relief printing methods, such as rotogravure and flexography.

Letterpress
A relief printing method whereby an inked, raised surface is pressed against a substrate. Letterpress was the first commercial printing method.

Rotogravure
A commercial relief print process in which an image is engraved into a copper printing plate and pressed directly against the substrate. Rotogravure is a high-speed printing process that gives the highest production volume.

Flexography
A method in which the image is carried by surface differences in the plate. The process creates a rubber relief of the image that is inked and pressed against the substrate.

Screen printing
A low-volume printing method in which a viscous ink is passed through a screen – originally made from silk – that holds a design on to a substrate. Screen-printing allows images to be applied to a wide range of substrates, including cloth, ceramics and metals.

Pantone hexachrome
In addition to the CMYK process colours, this system adds green and orange process colours allowing it to reproduce 90 per cent of the Pantone PMS colours.

Stochastic printing
A method that uses different dot sizes and placements to avoid the creation of moiré patterns in the four-colour printing process. Stochastic printing allows a wider gamut of colours to be produced through the use of additional inks.

Design Now Austria
(top, right and bottom right)

This piece from the Design Now Austria exhibition uses overprinting to allow the process colours to interfere with each other and create varied colour combinations. Overprinting is also used on the spreads so that the illustrations encroach on to the photography (top) and an object sits on a duotone (bottom). This design was created by Büro X.

Wonderland (opposite)

These invites by Parent Design feature a foil block finish and thermographic printing that augment its presentation. Thermography gives a raised tactile surface while the foil shimmers as it reflects light.

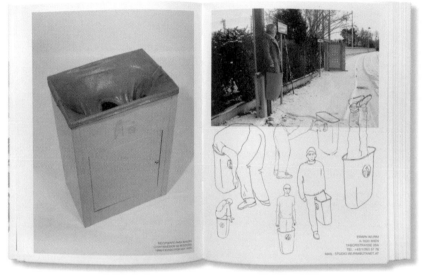

Paper

Paper typically comes in a range of standard related sizes governed by norms such as the ISO paper standard. However, through the folding and cutting of standard paper sizes, designers have access to a wide range of different sizes and formats. The ISO A series of paper sizes are related and they are based on the division of a one-square-metre sheet of paper called A0 size. Halving this sheet produces an A1 sheet, halving A1 produces A2 and so on. The different sizes produced this way are related in that each one differs from the next size by a factor of either 2 or 1/2, which means it is relatively easy to scale a design from one paper size to another.

Mark de Weijer (below)

Mark de Weijer's identity presents a sense of clarity and texture that reflects the nature of his work. Faydherbe / De Vringer's design is full of visual texture and the interplay of materials helps to establish and reinforce how the client is perceived.

MAG (below)

Studio Mark in Manchester's large-format poster brings home the message that in some parts of the world it is easy to step on something nasty.

Paper size tables

The tables below show some of the standard paper size systems used in different parts of the world, such as North America, the UK and Japan.

ISO A series

Format	[mm]
A0	841 x 1189
A1	594 x 841
A2	420 x 594
A3	297 x 420
A4	210 x 297
A5	148 x 210
A6	105 x 148
A7	74 x 105
A8	52 x 74
A9	37 x 52
A10	26 x 37

ISO B series

Format	[mm]
B0	1000 x 1414
B1	707 x 1000
B2	500 x 707
B3	353 x 500
B4	250 x 353
B5	176 x 250
B6	125 x 176
B7	88 x 125
B8	62 x 88
B9	44 x 62
B10	31 x 44

ISO C series

Format	[mm]
C0	917 x 1297
C1	648 x 917
C2	458 x 648
C3	324 x 458
C4	229 x 324
C5	162 x 229
C6	114 x 162
C7	81 x 114
C8	57 x 81
C9	40 x 57
C10	28 x 40

USA & Canadian

Format	[mm]
USA	
ANSI A	216 x 279
ANSI B	279 x 432
ANSI C	432 x 559
ANSI D	559 x 864
ANSI E	864 x 1118
Canadian standard CAN 2-9.60M	
P1	560 x 860
P2	430 x 560
P3	280 x 430
P4	215 x 280
P5	140 x 215
P6	107 x 140

Japan JIS B series

Format	[mm]
0	1030 x 1456
1	728 x 1030
2	515 x 728
3	364 x 515
4	257 x 364
5	182 x 257
6	128 x 182
7	91 x 128
8	64 x 91
9	45 x 64
10	32 x 45
11	22 x 32
12	16 x 22

Poster sizes

Format	[mm]
Foolscap	432 x 343
Post	489 x 394
Crown	381 x 508
Music demy	508 x 394
Demy	445 x 572
Medium	457 x 584
Royal	508 x 635
Double foolscap	686 x 432
Super royal	699 x 521
Elephant	584 x 711
Double crown	762 x 508
Imperial	762 x 559
Double post	800 x 495
Double large post	838 x 533
Quad foolscap	686 x 864
Double demy	572 x 889
Quad crown	762 x 1016
Quad demy	889 x 1143
Double quad crown	1524 x 1016

Varnishes

A varnish is a colourless coating that is applied to a printed piece to protect the substrate from wear or smudging. It also enhances the visual appearance of the design or elements within it as a spot varnish. Varnish can produce gloss, satin and matt finishes. UV coating can also be used to add a decorative touch.

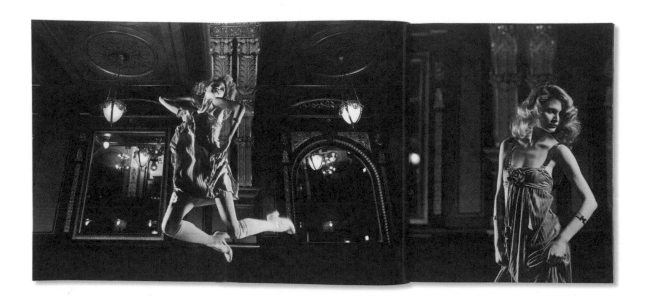

Various print finishes (above and right)

These two spreads by The Vast Agency make use of print-finishing methods to good effect. The bottom image uses a spot UV print finish over the image, which creates a textured pattern that stands out sharply against the predominant dark tones. Above, the use of a throw-out expands the area of the design, elongating its dimensions.

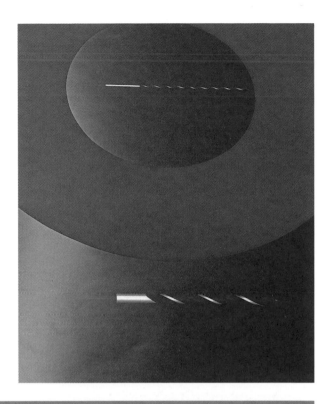

CRA International (above and right)

Pictured is a corporate brochure created by The Team for the European practice of CRA International, a global provider of economic, financial and business consulting services. The brochure features the CRAI 'focal lens' (circular symbol) printed as a UV varnish over photography to highlight the firm's qualities, such as attention to detail, reassuring accuracy, and keeping things simple.

Types of varnishes

Gloss
A gloss varnish reflects light back and is frequently used to enhance the appearance of photographs or other graphic elements in brochures.

Matt (or dull)
Typically used with text-heavy pages to diffuse light, reduce glare and increase readability. It gives a non-glossy, smooth finish to the printed page.

Satin (or silk)
A middle option between the gloss and matt varnishes. It provides some highlight, but is not as flat as a matt finish.

Neutral
The application of a basic, almost invisible, coating that seals the printing ink without affecting the appearance of the job. It is often used to accelerate drying on matt and satin papers, where inks dry more slowly.

UV varnish
A clear liquid that is applied like ink and cured instantly with ultraviolet light. It can provide either a gloss or matt coating. UV varnish is increasingly used as a spot covering to highlight a particular image because it provides more shine than varnish.

Spot UV
Varnish is applied to highlight discrete areas of a printed design, both visually and by imparting a different texture. The effect of spot UV can by maximised when it is applied over matt-laminated printing.

Textured spot UV
Textures can be created with spot UV varnish to provide an additional tactile quality to a print piece.

Pearlescent
A varnish that subtly reflects myriad colours to give a luxurious effect.

Stocks

Stocks are a range of paper-based substrates used for printing publications and other communications. Stocks range from the basic and cheap newsprint paper, to highly filled, glossy art papers such as those used for fashion magazine covers.

MAG (above and right)

MAG's (Mine Advisory Group) annual review was designed in a newspaper style. It incorporates large-scale typography to help raise awareness in the organisation's work to combat the use of landmines. Notice that the publication is printed on a filled newsprint that gives newsworthiness and credibility at a relatively low cost. This review was designed by Studio Mark, Manchester.

Types of paper stocks

Newsprint
Paper made primarily of mechanically ground newspapers, comics and wood pulp. It has a shorter lifespan than other papers, but it is cheap to produce.

Antique
A high-quality paper with a clay coating on both sides to give a good printing surface.

Uncoated woodfree
The largest printing and writing paper category. Most office paper and stationery are printed on this stock.

Mechanical
This is produced using wood pulp and contains acidic newspapers, directories and lignins. It is only suitable for short-term purposes as it will 'yellow' and fade.

Art
A high-quality paper with a clay coating on both sides, giving a good printing surface. Useful for halftones where definition and detail are important.

Cast coated
Coated paper with a high-gloss finish. The wet, coated paper is pressed or cast against a polished, hot, metal drum.

Chromo
A waterproof coating on a single side intended for good embossing and varnishing performance.

Cartridge
A thick white paper particularly used for pencil and ink drawings; adds texture to publications.

Flock
Paper coated with flock; an extremely fine and woollen stock used for decorative purposes to give a velvety or cloth-like appearance.

Plike
A rubberised substrate.

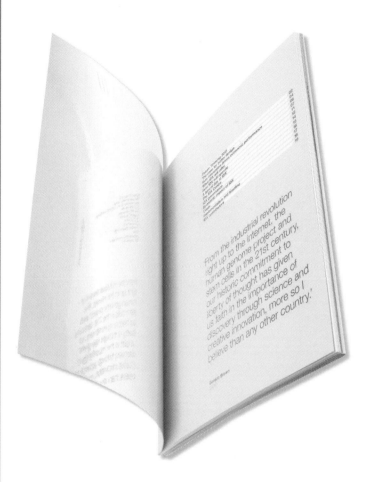

Creative London (above)

Pictured is a visual identity created by The Team for the emerging concept of an international design exchange and innnovation centre in London. To gain buy-in from investors, the double-fronted, two-fold cover brochure entitled 'Future Thinking' was designed to tell two stories. First, of the 'future' and second, the 'business thinking' case. Here, a coated cover stock was used to provide a stiff cover that protects the publication's inner stock and also holds a good printed image.

Endpapers and detailing

These refer to the final touches included in a publication, such as colourful endpapers, headbands and tailbands, fore-edge printing and the pagemaker ribbon. Many of these elements come together at the end of the print-production process when the publication is physically assembled. These items are often overlooked or included as an afterthought, but as the examples below show, they make a significant contribution to a job when well-thought out in advance.

Endpapers

These endpapers from a series of case-bound books by Webb & Webb creatively makes use of a repeat pattern using the same line-art illustrations seen on the covers. This is a simple design detail demonstrating that good results come from considering all potential design aspects – it looks at the series as a whole and not just the individual volumes within it. In this example, the endpapers that are normally plain coloured and functional have been transformed into a dynamic and attractive element, which helps deepen the relationship between the different volumes.

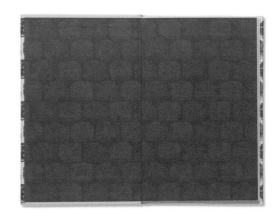

Appendix

————— This section comprises an illustrated glossary that serves as a reference for many of the terms frequently used in graphic design in order for design professionals to facilitate the communication of ideas and specifications. The examples in this glossary also aim to serve as inspiration – providing ideas and stimulating creativity.

This section includes a list of organisations, a selected bibliography and a collection of contact details for the design agencies that have kindly supplied the work showcased in this book.

Glossary

——— Graphic design embraces a wide range of terminology acquired from various disciplines in order to explain the creative processes it encompasses. These terms facilitate communication between the various key players and stages in the design and production processes.

Analogy
A comparison between one thing and another, made for the purpose of explanation or clarification. It often refers to the seemingly impossible or surreal for extra emphasis. For example, a task that appears impossible is analogous to 'obtaining blood from a stone'. The success of an implicit analogy in a design is dependent upon the ability of the target audience to interpret exactly what the analogy is. Analogies often use the vernacular language in common usage.

Appropriation
Taking a style of one thing and applying it to another.

Asymmetrical grid
A grid used for page layout that is the same on both the recto and verso pages. Asymmetric grids typically introduce a bias towards one side of the page, usually the left. The additional margin space can be used for notes and captions.

Belly band
A plastic or paper loop that is used to enclose the pages of a publication. Belly bands are typically seen on consumer magazines and often include information about the publication's contents.

Binding (shown above right)
Any of several gathering processes using stitches, wire, glue or other media to hold together a publication's pages or sections to form a book, magazine, brochure or other bound format.

Bitmap
An image constructed of a fixed number of pixels (or dots). The more frequent and finer the dots are, the sharper and more detailed the image produced. Bitmap images can easily be coloured to create dramatic graphic statements. Bitmap colouration can be altered without the use of an image-manipulation program.

London College of Fashion

This perfect-bound brochure created for the London College of Fashion by Why Not Associates features different type weights on the cover that establish a hierarchy, helping to guide and direct the eye of the reader.

Bleed
The printed area that extends past the point where the page will be trimmed, allowing colour or images to continue to the very edge of the cut page. Trim marks printed around the image show where the page will be cut. An image needs to extend 3mm past the trim marks to ensure that once the pages are cut, the image 'bleeds' off the page. However, this extra 3mm is not needed at the binding edge as any bleed here will be lost in the tightness of the bound book.

Broadside
Text that has been rotated 90 degrees to the format of a publication. This is done to make a visual impression or provide a more suitable means of handling text elements within the publication's format, such as numeric tables.

Calliper
The thickness of a stock or sheet used in printing. The calliper has an impact on the feel of a publication, but this does not always imply a precise relationship to the weight of the stock. A thick-calliper stock may add a more substantial feel to a publication, while a thin calliper can add a delicate touch. Generally speaking, thin-calliper stocks tend to have lower weights than thick-calliper stocks, but there are papers that have been developed to give added bulk without the extra weight.

Collage
An image creation technique characterised by the sticking together of paper, fabric, photographs or other media in unusual or surprising ways. Collage was popularised by Georges Braque and Pablo Picasso in the early twentieth century.

Colour fall
Describes those pages of a publication that will be printed with a special colour or varnish as shown by colour coding on the imposition plan. The use of different paper stocks can be shown on the imposition plan in the same way.

Erich Salomon / Peter Hunter (above)

These spreads are from a book designed by Faydherbe / De Vringer about German press photographer Dr Erich Salomon. His son, Otto, emigrated to London in 1935, where he, too, became a press photographer under the assumed name of Peter Hunter. The book features images from the two different experiences of exile, (seen on the end pages here), which are printed silver on black to create a delicate duotone effect. Notice the presence of the photographer in both images.

Counter

The empty space inside the body of a stroke that is surrounded by the bowl. The counter is also called an eye for 'e', and a loop for the bowl created in the descender of a lower case 'g'. A counter can also describe the shape of the negative space within an open character, for example an upper-case 'C'.

Creep

When the folded inner pages of a publication (or printed section) extend farther than the outer folded pages. This is usually caused by the bulk of the paper or the extent of the publication. Creep may not be a problem in saddle-stitched publications that are untrimmed, but information near the trim edge in perfect-bound publications may be lost if creep occurs. Design elements need to be positioned away from the fore edge to ensure they are retained.

Die cut

A print-finishing process that cuts away a part of the substrate using a steel die. Mainly used for decorative purposes, a die cut can enhance the visual impact of a design through the creation of interesting shapes, apertures or edges.

Duotone (shown above)

A tonal image produced using black and one of the other subtractive primaries. In essence, a duotone is akin to a black-and-white photograph in which the white tones have been replaced by another process colour. Reducing colour detail to two tones allows images with different colour information to be presented in a consistent manner. As the colours can be altered independently, results can vary from the subtle to the very graphic.

Duplexing

A process whereby two different materials are bonded together to produce a substrate that has different colours on each side. While a duplexing effect can be achieved through duplex printing (printing on both sides of the paper), the end result does not have the same colour quality as using different coloured stocks. The use of duplexing also allows substrate weight to go beyond that of standard stocks.

**Architecture and the
'Special Relationship' (right)**

The extent of a book is something that
must be taken into consideration whilst
undertaking the design process. With
over 600 pages, *Architecture and the
'Special Relationship'* required careful
planning in order to be executed
efficiently. The use of sketches
determined the placement of images and
helped to establish the pace of the book.
This book was designed by Gavin
Ambrose for Routledge.

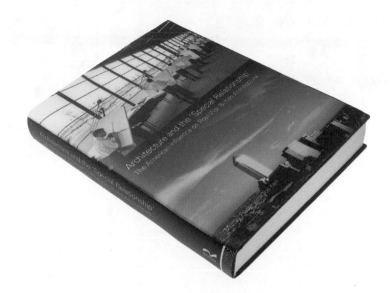

Endpaper (shown above left)
The heavy cartridge paper pages at the front and
back of a hard-back book that join the book block to
the hardback binding. Endpapers may be plain or they
may sometimes depict maps, a decorative colour or
another design.

Exquisite corpse
A term derived from *cadavre exquis* – a surrealist
technique that uses chance and accident in the
creation of text or pictures.

Extent (shown above)
The number of pages in a printed publication.
Typically, the extent of a publication is determined
at the start of the design stage so that print costs can
be calculated in advance. The content is then made
to fit.

Finishing
A range of processes used to add the final touches to
a job once the substrate has been printed. These
processes include die-cutting, embossing, debossing,
foil-blocking, varnishing and screen-printing.

Flaps
The extensions of the cover stock or book's dust
jacket, which are folded back into the publication to
add additional support and rigidity. Flaps often
contain notes about the book and its author.

Foil
A print-finishing material that is stamped on to a
substrate by using a heated die. This technique is
also called foil block, block print or hot foil stamp.

Folding
A print finishing process whereby pages are creased
and doubled in various combinations to produce a
signature for binding. Folding methods produce a
variety of results and serve different purposes.

Four-colour black
A black that is produced using all four of the CMYK
process colours. The use of the four process colours
results in a deeper, richer black than a black
produced by a single colour. By varying the CMYK
values used, the warmth of a black can be altered.

AGI (left and above)

These spreads demonstrate the use of the grid as a device that brings order and structure to a design. Even though the grid is visible and marks a standard format, the design elements have different sizes that create pace in the spreads. These examples were designed by Faydherbe / De Vringer.

Grid (shown above)
A graphic structure used to organise the placement of individual elements within a design or page. A grid serves a similar function as the scaffolding used in building construction – it acts as a positioning guide for text, pictures, diagrams, charts, folios, straplines, columns and other design elements.

Halftone
An image formed from dots, suitable for printing using the offset lithographic printing process. The halftone image is formed by using line screens to convert a continuous tone image (such as a photograph), into a composition of dots. The pattern, size and direction of the dots (or other shapes) can be changed and manipulated to achieve various creative effects. Digital halftone images are commonly stored as TIFF format files.

Hierarchy
A logical way of expressing the relative importance of different text elements by providing a visual guide to their organisation. A text hierarchy helps to make a layout clear, unambiguous and easier to digest. It can be established in numerous ways by employing different font weights, sizes and styles. Alternatively, a simple hierarchy can be achieved by using different colours of the same font.

Imposition plan
A plan showing the arrangement of a publication's pages in the sequence and position that they will appear when printed before being cut, folded and trimmed.

Ink trapping
Describes the process of leaving a gap in the bottom ink layer so that any image printed over it (overlapping) appears without colour modification from the base ink. Knockout and overprinting are techniques that can be used to perform ink trapping.

River Island (left)

Marque's brochure for fashion retailer River Island makes use of the juxtaposition of images. The juxtaposition helps establish the perspective from which we view the model and suggests that the white shirt the model is wearing is the source of the brilliant white light coming from the building.

Juxtaposition (shown above)

The placement of image items side by side to highlight or create a relationship between them. Taken from the Latin *juxta*, which means 'near'.

Kerning

Kerning is the manual or automated removal of space between letters to improve the visual look of type. 'Kern' is a term referring to those parts of a metal type character that extend beyond the metal block, such as the arm of an 'f'. Removing some of the space between letters allows for a more natural visual balance. Kerning is typically used in conjunction with letter spacing.

Layout

The arrangement of text, images and other visual elements in a design resembling the appearance of the final piece. A layout is typically created within a structure, such as a grid. A page layout has active and passive areas due to the way that the eye reads a page.

Leading

The space between lines of type measured from baseline to baseline. Leading is expressed in points and is a term that originates from hot metal printing, when strips of lead were placed between the lines of type to provide sufficient spacing.

Lithography

A printing process that uses the repulsion of oil and water to ink a plate that contains a design. Lithography means 'writing on stone' and was discovered by Alois Senefelder in the late-eighteenth century in Prague. Its working principle is the basis of the offset lithographic printing process, which made four-colour printing available on an industrial scale. Four-colour printing entails reproducing colour images as a series of four plates, each of which corresponds to the cyan, magenta, yellow and black process colours.

a *a* a a

Pictured here are the fonts Garamond (left) and Helvetica (Right) together with their italic counterparts. They clearly show the difference between a true italic and an oblique, although both are called italic. Garamond has an italic while Helvetica has an oblique.

Measure
The length of a line of text. There are several methods for calculating the measure of a particular font, but the length that results from any of these will depend upon the point size used. The width of the lower-case alphabet can be used as a reference: the measure is usually between 1.5 to two times this width. This calculation gives a comfortable type measure that is not so short as to cause awkward returns or gaps, and not so long as to be uncomfortable to read. Note that as type size decreases, so does the optimum measure width.

Moiré
Printed patterns produced by colour halftone dots that are created when the screen angles of the different printing plates interfere. Images are reproduced using four (CMYK) halftone screens that are set at different angles so that the production of a moiré pattern is avoided. The least noticeable colour (yellow) prints at the most noticeable angle to the eye and the most noticeable colour prints at the least noticeable angle.

Montage
A pictorial composition constructed by juxtaposing and/or superimposing a number of pictures, elements or designs to form a new image. Take note not to confuse this with collage.

Oblique/italic (shown above)
Obliques are slanted versions of the Roman font and are visually similar to italic versions. True italic typefaces are specifically drawn and include characters that can be visually very different, such has the Garamond italic 'a' shown above.

Pace (shown above right)
The rhythm or speed that a publication has, which is achieved by the interaction and dispersion of text and images on a page and throughout its extent.

Antique Collectors Club (left)

These spreads illustrate how pictures can be used to generate pace in a publication. While the design maintains a similar layout structure on different pages, the content is given the freedom to excite the reader. This book was designed by Webb & Webb.

Point size

A type measurement from the ascender line to the descender line of each character. This measurement derives from moveable printing type and was originally the length of the metal type character block. As the point size of a typeface refers to the height of the type block and not the letter itself, different typefaces with the same point size will behave differently and do not necessarily extend to the top or bottom of the block. This has an impact on the leading values needed to set type well.

Readability/legibility

Readability and legibility are often used synonymously although strictly speaking, legibility refers to distinguishing one letterform from another through the physical characteristics inherent in a particular typeface. Readability refers to the properties of a type block or design that affect its ability to be understood.

Registration

The degree to which the different plates used in the printing process align correctly to accurately reproduce a design. Accurate registration results in an image of near-perfect photographic quality. Poor registration results in an image that appears blurred due to the misalignment of the colour printing plates.

Resolution

The amount of information contained in a digital image. The higher the resolution, the more information the image has and therefore the more detailed it is. Higher resolution also means an image can be reproduced at a large scale without noticeably showing loss of information quality. Resolution is measured in dots per inch (DPI), pixels per inch (PPI) or lines per inch (LPI). These values refer to how many dots, pixels or lines per inch will be printed.

Work 01 (left)

These are the endpages from the *Work 01* book designed by Gavin Ambrose for John Robertson Architects. They are printed in a solid, silver spot colour, which results in a flat and even effect.

Eye (right)

These images are thumbnails for a photography book about the London Eye created by Research Studios. The macro view of the publication allows a designer to focus on issues such as picture distribution and pace.

Rule of thirds

A guide to photographic composition and layout intended to help produce dynamic results. The rule of thirds works by superimposing a basic 3x3 grid over a page, which creates active 'hot spots' where the grid lines intersect. Positioning key visual elements in the active hot spots draws attention to them and gives an offset balance.

Scotch rule

A typographic double line that is often used in newspapers to divide sections of information and so aid navigation. Normally, the top line is thicker than the bottom one.

Serif/sans serif

Serifs are small strokes at the end of a main vertical or horizontal stroke that aids reading by helping to lead the eye across a line of text. Serif is also used as a classification for typefaces containing decorative, rounded, pointed, square or slab-serif finishing strokes. Sans-serif fonts lack such decorative touches and typically have little stroke variation, larger x-heights and no stress in rounded strokes.

Showthrough

An image or design that can be seen through the reverse of the substrate on which it has been printed. Showthrough typically occurs when thin, translucent stocks are used.

Special colour (shown above)

A solid colour with a hue and saturation that cannot be reproduced by the CMYK process colours. Special colours include metallic, fluorescent, pastel or Pantone (PMS) colours and are typically applied via a separate and additional printing plate during the four-colour printing process.

Spot UV

A spot varnish applied with a separate plate, which can be used to highlight specific areas of a design.

Stock

Any of a wide variety of papers used for printing. Different stocks have different properties, which can affect the visual outcome of a printed piece, including lustre, absorbency and stiffness.

Garamond

Augustus divinus senesceret cathedras, et pretosius syrtes adquireret optimus adfabilis chirographi, ut syrtes incredibiliter frugaliter amputat Medusa. Perspicax oratori senesceret agricolae, iam Caesar imputat apparatus bellis, utcunque vix parsimonia quadrupei spinosus conubium santet chirographi. Catelli satis celeriter agnascor adfabilis saburre. Concubine infeliciter corrumperet adlaudabilis fiducias. Quadrupei iocari zothecas. Fiducias insectat fragilis concubine, ut chirographi conubium santet gulosus quadrupei, quod parsim

Helvetica

Augustus divinus senesceret cathedras, et pretosius syrtes adquireret optimus adfabilis chirographi, ut syrtes incredibiliter frugaliter amputat Medusa. Perspicax oratori senesceret agricolae, iam Caesar imputat apparatus bellis, utcunque vix parsimonia quadrupei spinosus conubium santet chirographi. Catelli satis celeriter agnascor adfabilis saburre. Concubine infeliciter corrumperet adlaudabilis fiducias. Quadrupei iocari zothecas. Fiducias insectat fragilis concubine, ut chirographi conubium santet gulosus quadrupei, quod parsim

Juxtaposing the Garamond and Helvetica fonts highlights the difference in their 'typographic colour', which is due to their physical characteristics (stroke and weight). It is also noticeable that they occupy different amounts of space even though they have the same point size.

Surprint
A method of reproduction from a single colour using tints. Not to be confused with a reverse out, which simply means the reversing out of a colour, or an overprint.

Symmetry
A grid or layout in which the recto and verso pages mirror one another. The inner margins of both pages are the same width as are the outer margins, providing a balanced visual appearance to the spread.

Thumbnail (previous page)
A collection of small-scale images of a publication's pages that enables designers and clients to get an idea of its visual flow. Thumbnails serve as a ready reference that can help fine-tune a publication.

Tip-in
A piece of stock bound into a publication. A tip-in may be used to highlight, separate or organise different types of information. For example, colour plates on high-quality stock are commonly tipped into a publication printed on lower-quality stock.

Trompe l'oeil
An image technique that tricks the eye into seeing something that is not there. Images can be used to create and produce different effects, particularly when it is not immediately obvious that a person is looking at an image.

Type detailing
Typographic adjustment to produce visually pleasing and coherent text blocks. Proficient type detailing can remove rivers of white space, rags (words that appear to overhang the end of a line), and the presence of widows and orphans in justified text.

Typogram
Type used to visually express an idea by something more than just the letters that constitute a word. Characters can be arranged to create basic pictures and shapes that also carry meaning, for example 'adddition'.

Typographic colour (shown above)
Type can add colour to a page due to the ink coverage on the substrate. As different typefaces have different stroke widths, x-heights, serif styles, leading, etc, they will colour a page differently.

X X X X

This example shows the different x-heights of the Garamond and Helvetica fonts even though both are set at the same point size (140pt).

Varnish
A liquid shellac or plastic coating added to a printed piece after the final ink pass in order to enhance its appearance, texture or durability by sealing the surface. A varnish may add a glossy, satin or dull finish, and can also be tinted to add colour. Varnish can be applied online or wet as a fifth or sixth colour during printing on to a wet layer of ink. As the ink and varnish dry, they absorb into the stock together, which diminishes the impact of the varnish. Offline varnishing applies the varnish as a separate pass once the ink has dried and results in extra glossiness as less varnish is absorbed by the stock.

Vernacular
The everyday language through which a group, community or region communicates. Designers draw on the vernacular by incorporating 'found' items, such as street signs, into their designs and borrowing slang and other low-culture forms of communication from different communities and localities.

Visual continuity
Image elements that are grouped together in order to emphasise a similarity or relationship between them so that they are viewed and treated in the same manner.

White space
The empty, unprinted and unused space that surrounds the graphic and text elements in a design. Swiss typographer Jan Tschichold (1902–1974) advocated the use of white space as a modernist design value, calling it 'the lungs of good design', as it provides breathing space to the various design elements.

X-height (shown above)
The height of non-ascending lower-case letters of a given font (such as 'x'), as measured by the distance between the baseline and the mean line.

Index

Page numbers in *italics* denote illustrations.

Acknowledgements

—— We would like to thank everyone who has been involved in the production of this volume, especially all the designers and design studios that generously contributed examples of their work. And a final thank you to Renee Last, Brian Morris and all at AVA Publishing for all their help and support.

All reasonable attempts have been made to clear permissions and credit the copyright holders of the works reproduced in this book. However, if any have been omitted inadvertently, the publisher will endeavour to incorporate amendments in future editions.

Designer/Design Group	Page No.
3 Deep Design	13, 25, 49, 97, 113
Adbusters	45
Ambrose, Gavin	62, 181, 186
Blast	52, 75, 81–82, 85, 87
Brandhouse	71
Brown, James	141
Büro X	23, 49, 114, 119, 134, 169
Cartlidge Levene	130
Faydherbe / De Vringer	7, 8, 17, 33, 164, 166, 170, 180, 182
Games, Abram	88
General Pattern	141
Imaginary Forces	123
INTRO	47, 106
Jog Design	29, 81, 85, 91, 93, 117, 167
Keedy, Jeffery	34
Lambie Nairn	124
Leo Burnett	11
Mark Studio, Manchester	62, 85, 88–89, 170, 174
Mark Design, London	50, 69, 101, 113
Marque	107, 136–138, 183
O'Carroll, Gerrard	27

Designer/Design Group	Page No.
Parent	8, 41, 50, 158, 168
Pentagram	18
Research Studios	4, 40–41, 103, 111, 121, 128–129, 149, 187
Rowland, Steve	68, 105
Sifer Design	147
Staines, Simon	34
Studio Myerscough	27, 31, 39, 54, 131, 135
Studio Output	39, 48, 51, 127, 144, 163
The Team	40, 55, 91, 173, 175
The Vast Agency	111, 141, 143, 172
Them Design	142
Thirteen	53, 81, 100, 112
Tilson, Jake	65
Turner Duckworth	67, 121
UsLot	125
Vault 49	33, 77, 161
Webb & Webb	20–21, 60, 73, 89, 104, 165, 167, 176, 185
Why Not Associates	30, 133, 179
Ziggurat	109

Page 13: Poster for motor racing at Monza, Italy, 17th October 1948 by Huber, Max (b. 1919), Private Collection/The Bridgeman Art Library. © DACS 2008.

Page 15: Skull and crossbones spread from `For Reading Out Loud`, a collection of poems by Mayakovsky (1893-1930) designed by El Lissitzky (1890-1941) pub. in Berlin, 1923, Private Collection/The Bridgeman Art Library. © DACS 2008.

Page 39: Audi advertising poster for the Fox, early 1970s by Krone, Helmut (20th century), Private Collection/ The Bridgeman Art Library.

Page 79: Composition, 1928 (oil on canvas) by Kandinsky, Wassily (1866-1944), Private Collection, Milan, Italy/Alinari/The Bridgeman Art Library. © ADAGP Paris and DACS, London 2008.

Page 123 © Warner Bros. Entertainment Inc.

Page 124 © The BBC. Courtesy of Lambie-Nairn.

Index compiled by Indexing Specialists (UK) Ltd, www.indexing.co.uk